Stories of Love,
Awareness and Acceptance
on the Spectrum

Very mediocre

FOR THE
L♥VE
OF AUTISM

TAMIKA LECHEÉ MORALES
Foreword by Dr. Kerry Magro EdD

1

FOR THE LOVE OF AUTISM

© Copyright 2022, Tamika Lecheé Morales
All rights reserved.

No portion of this book may be reproduced by mechanical, photographic, or electronic process, nor may it be stored in a retrieval system, transmitted in any form, or otherwise be copied for public use or private use without written permission of the copyright owner.

This book is a compilation of stories from numerous people who have each contributed a chapter and is designed to provide inspiration to our readers.

It is sold with the understanding that the publisher and the individual authors are not engaged in the rendering of psychological, legal, accounting, or other professional advice. The content and views in each chapter are the sole expression and opinion of its author and not necessarily the views of Fig Factor Media, LLC.

For more information, contact:

Tamika Lecheé Morales | www.fortheloveofautism.com
Fig Factor Media, LLC | www.figfactormedia.com

Cover Design & Layout by LDG Juan Manuel Serna Rosales

Printed in the United States of America

ISBN: 978-1-952779-59-6
Library of Congress Control Number: 2022905935

This book is dedicated to *"The Legendary Kid"*, who has taught me more than I could ever teach him. Maximilian *Eros* Morales you are my world, my love, my everything. Thank you for making me all that I am and all that I never knew I could be.

-Mami

To those who need these stories: This is for you.

This book also is dedicated to a world that is too blind to see, too noisy to hear, and too slow to change. If you wake up tomorrow, it's still not too late.

-Tamika Lecheé Morales

TABLE OF CONTENTS

ACKNOWLEDGMENTS

If there's anything that I have learned, it's that we aren't meant to go through life alone! The African proverb got it right: "If you want to go fast, go alone. If you want to go far, go together."

Sometimes we read to know that we are not alone. YOU are not alone and thankfully neither am I. This book is a labor of love and I have so many people to thank for it. The reality that this book is here today is because of those who have been by my side in different seasons, who have invested and poured into me when my own cup was low. I am better because of them. So, it is with a full heart that I am grateful to each and every one of you.

First and foremost: Thank you, God, for being omnipotent, omniscient, omnipresent, and omnibenevolent. You delivered me from the darkness and brought me back into the light where I belong. Help me to stay here like only you can. #GodIsGrand

To my moms, Mom and *Mami:* We all are paying for the sins of our fathers. There have been generational curses bestowed upon us, but both of you have done your best to break these cycles. Our parenting is not perfect, but we are not perfect. Thank you for doing the best you could. I never felt a shortage of love. You loved me unconditionally and that's what matters. Your love and belief in me keep me strong. Thank you for all I am and all I hope to be. *Te quiero con todo.* #NothingLikeAMothersLove

Hugo Boss: You get the award. I really don't know how the hell you do it, but you do it with such patience and grace. Thank you for all the grace you extend to me. God knows you have endured the good, the bad, and the ugly, and you haven't left. You are the proof that God has not forsaken me. Without you, I wouldn't be me. We have our own kind of love story. With big red puckered duck lips . . . *Yo nací para amarte*, 'til death do we part. And maybe not even then. You should be so lucky. #TuCielo

Dear sons (*Lobo Blanco* and The Legendary Kid): Lose your fears, not your confidence. Make meaning of your existence. Know that my love has no limits and that you inspire me each and every day. You are my greatest accomplishments, and I have been blessed by being your mom. Legendary Kid, this book is for you and other unique humans like you. #BeTrueToYou

Brother and Sister (Darnell & Jessica): You get praises just for being blood. I adore you both, and the morning pics of the little humans you've created really do start my day off with a smile. Keep them coming and remind them always how much *titi* loves them. Love you guys. Maybe one of these days we can finally get it together and not live so many miles apart. #FamilyGoals

Jeanette Miranda: Thank you for being a faithful friend, confidant, cheerleader, and soundboard. Thank you for your encouragement and prayers. Most of all, thank you for your friendship. You planted the seed for this anthology on September 27, 2020, and we can celebrate together now that it is here! Love ya, girl. #RenaissanceChica

To the authors: I cannot express the gratitude in my heart that you said "yes" to me, to this project, and to its mission. Thank you for coming together as ONE voice to educate the masses and to unify for the greater good. I have learned so much about resilience from your stories; but most of all, I have learned that even in adversity there is a gift. Each and every one of you has been a gift to me. Luv you all. #FTLAAuthors

Eileen Lamb (The Autism Cafe): You, my friend, get an extra special shout-out. You were the first influencer I contacted and without hesitation, you listened, heard, and helped. I admire your courage. The world needs more Eileens. You truly are special. Don't ever change. *Je vous aime. Merci.* #TheAutismCafe

My posse Luz Quagliaroli (Lulu), Rachel Lamboy (even in death you are with me), Gloria Lamboy, Michelle Gerez (Chela), Gabriela Quevedo, *Familia* Cuevas, Isabel Torres, Teresa Santiago, Evelyn Sanchez-Toledo, Judy Rivera, Jacqueline Cardona (Jackster), Jeanette Segui, Patricia Alcala (Tisha), Marisa Muñoz, Leticia Neri (even from heaven), Marilynn Lopez, Gisenia Diaz, Yanira Guzman, Astrid Rivera, Esperanza Ortiz, Mercedes Feliz-Matos, Marina Kostina, David Lopez, Lila Navarro, Analiz and Veronica Molina, Shama Malik, Reinette Carrico, Shawn Fair, and Milton Otero: There are friends, there is family, and then there are friends that become family. Because of you I laugh a little harder, cry a little less, and smile a lot more. #MyTribe

To my heroes past and present at The Autism Hero Project (AHP)—Jaime Clark, Angelica Silva, Marcus Williams, Michelle Kapusta, Sylvia Garcia, Deborah Wilbert, Deborah Ann Hines, Mike Oquendo, George Theodossopoulos, Jen Schleicher, Mary Jane Battaglia, Felix Sanchez, Juan Graciani, Enrique Mendoza, Jose Birriel, Chavdar Angelov, Jennifer Lewis, Megan Carranza, Ava Hawkins, Karina Guzman, Kimberly Johnson, Samantha Rojek, Christina Hernandez, Madison Hernandez, Susan Kerrigan-Barnett, and so many more: I wish I could name you all, but we would never get to the rest of the book. Thank you! You do HEROES work every day because you know the compounding effect: little by little, a little becomes a lot. Together we are changing the world for someone we love. #StrongerTogether #AutismHeroProject #NotAllHeroesWearCapes

My book sisters (*Today's Inspired Latina*), Daisy Jimenez, Yaneth Medina, Ana Santos-Vitelo, Luz Canino-Baker, Luz-Marie Caro, Dolly Rosario, Elizabeth Colón-Rivera, Marisel Melendez, Teresita Marsal Avila, Angelica Monroy, Maria Castro, Amanda Sanchez, Linda Alberty-Layhew, Gabriela Reyna, Carmina Cortes, Paloma Greer, Zory Martínez Jaen, Sandra Maldonado-Martinez, Mariela Camacho-Kimble, Ivys Ramirez, Jennifer Sanchez, Irma Zavala, Karen O'Donnell, Iris Soto, Minué Yoshida, Channabelle Arriaga, Tanya Flores, *y mucha más:* There is strength in sisterhood. When one of us rises, we all rise. #TodaysInspiredLatinas #PowerToTheSisters

Latinas United in Love for Autism (LULA), the originals plus some: I can't forget about you *chulas*. Liza Pereira, Mary Flores Rios, Evelyn Perez-Horita, Daisy Berrios, Denise Badillo, Annette Lugo, Cheva Ramos, Julissa Graciani, Isabel Gonzalez-Smith, Diana Sanchez, Vanessa Fawley, and the rest of the mommas. Thanks for being the safe space that we all needed. May we continue to learn, to grow and to be a resource to one another. #LULA

Fig Factor Media Dream Team: I cannot believe it! We did it! It's done! I can truly say that I could not have done this book without this AMAZING team. Anna Fisher, you have been a dream editor! From where we started to how we finished, we coined ourselves "sisters-in-editing." You really "understood the assignment" and it's going to be hard not texting, messaging, and exchanging emails morning, noon, and night as often as we did. You and Izar have gained a permanent place in my heart! Izar Olivares, your work was instrumental in this book . . . you have a way with words. Gaby Hernández Franch, thank you for always meeting my intensity with your peaceful aura. Your smile and pleasant demeanor are the secret weapon to always setting me at ease. You never say no, which makes you the worthiest of all author concierges ever! Juan Manuel Serna Rosales, I am privileged to have worked with you as my graphic design artist all of these years. You always meet me with a willingness to please. You don't quit until I think it's perfect, and for that I am so appreciative of you. Thank you for the beautiful book design. It's perfection.

Juan Pablo, you have a creative side that is unmatched. Anna Marie Kukec Tomczyk, my heart is full knowing that my proofreader is an award-winning journalist and author with a heart for marginalized communities and over thirty years of experience. #FigFactorMedia #DreamTeam.

Jacqueline Camacho-Ruiz: #Pilotina, there aren't words for what you mean to me but I'm gonna try. You are a #DreamCatcher, #MagiXMaker and a #MakeItHappen queen. My world changed the minute I met you. Thank you for coming into my life when you did. It's been an amazing ride. I can't wait to see what the future holds with you by my side. #PilotinaAndFiressa #SkysTheLimit

FOREWORD

"I want you to imagine something for a second. Imagine that you were unable to tell the people that you care about the most in this world that you love them. Imagine a situation where you wouldn't even be able to tell your loved ones about your basic needs. Imagine not being able to tell your dad that you were hungry or your mom that you were thirsty. For all intents and purposes, you were just there with no way of communicating with those around you. This used to be my reality."

If you told my parents that their son, who was nonspeaking till two-and-one-half years old, diagnosed with autism at four, and didn't speak in complete sentences until seven would years later be an author of several books on growing up autistic, I'm not sure they'd believe it.

Hello there. My name is Kerry, and I'm autistic and have dysgraphia; today, I am a professional speaker, author, and autism entertainment consultant. The quote above is from the second TEDx Talk I gave titled, "What Happens to Children with Autism When They Become Adults," where I discussed my autism journey. In the talk, I also discussed the importance of realizing autism doesn't end at the age of eighteen and the need to support autistics who have additional requirements across their lifespan.

When Tamika connected with me about writing the foreword to this book, I was instantly blown away by her dedication to autism. I was delighted to have an opportunity to continue writing forewords after writing two, one for an autistic pastor and one for an autistic artist and his mother.

I've had a passion for writing for many years. One of my first inspirations in joining the writing world was one of the first autism books I read in 2009. The book was *Look Me in the Eye: My Life with Asperger's* by John Elder Robison, an autistic adult raising an autistic son. At the time, it was the only book I knew about autism. However, reading about similar stories to my own made me feel less alone in the autism community. Fast forward to now, and we have more and more books coming out each day.

This is not just any book, though...

Not only is Tamika an actor, entrepreneur, writer, speaker, teacher, and president of The Autism Hero Project (AHP), but she is also the mom of an autistic son who she loves dearly. These are a few reasons why I believe this book can become a favorite of yours:

THE IMPORTANCE OF A VILLAGE

Tamika stood out to me right away when she said that she often found a divide in the autism community. Her hope, similar to my own, is to unite a society that has differing opinions. Eileen Lamb, an autistic adult, mother of an autistic son, and contributor to this book, has a great quote: "It seems like the best way to not offend an autism advocate is to say nothing at all, and that is the last thing we should be doing." I agree 100 percent with this sentiment. As I share in my chapter, I see this far too often as a self-advocate and consultant for parents. Autism is a spectrum—we have to understand that we all have a universal goal while disagreeing with one another. Regardless of whether we have a personal connection to autism or not, this goal is to progress, to live the best quality of life possible. That's why I applaud Tamika's involvement with contributors, who are both on the spectrum and not. It shows she understands the true definition of the word "village." When inclusion works, it's about bringing all of our collective voices together. It truly takes a village, and I'm happy to be part of the village that helped make this book a reality.

A LABOR OF LOVE

When writing this foreword, I thought about the title, *For the Love of Autism*, and at first thought of those memes on social media that say, "I love someone with autism" and also "I love someone with autism to the moon and back." I was constantly engaged by those, not just because they always get thousands of shares, but because of the stories I'd read from our autism community in the comments that often held the true definition of love. In the same way, Tamika's love for this community, the love for her son, and the love you will hear from the contributors, I'm sure, will resonate with many of you.

THE EDUCATION THIS BOOK BRINGS

One thing I advocate for as a professional speaker is the importance of moving from autism awareness to autism acceptance. We've been aware of autism for years, but there are people, such as myself who just want to be accepted for exactly who we are. Tamika's story is interesting because when she decided to start her own nonprofit, The Autism Hero Project (AHP), it brought great education about the importance of autism legislation and medical needs to our society. As a teacher, Tamika understands the importance of education, and, yes, while you may be inspired by the stories you'll read in this book, you also may learn a thing or two that you can use in your day-to-day life.

I could go on and on, but I want to take a second to thank you, the reader, and also thank Tamika for making this book a reality. And without further ado . . . Here's *For the Love of Autism.*

- Dr. Kerry Magro, EdD

INTRODUCTION

"In the absence of love and belonging,
there is always suffering."
–Brené Brown

Writing a book like this is like writing an extension of your soul. You do it for different reasons: to know that you are not alone, to connect, to forgive, to teach, to heal, or maybe to remember. Whatever the root of it is, you are the one who gets to define it. Maybe your story will connect with others, maybe they will see themselves in you.

You hope your story will resonate, so you slave over every word, you second guess, you dare to get vulnerable at the risk of exposing too much. Maybe in your attempt to explain your experiences you show the parts of you that you normally hide or, worse, you expose the people you love. You fear that your words may later haunt you, so you pause, set boundaries, erase, retreat, then return and write some more, read, edit, and write again until you think it is ready. You don't want to hurt anyone with your words because you know that words have power. Once published, they can never be erased. To write is to be brave. And I commend these authors for showing up with bravery.

Brené Brown shares that "The biggest myth about vulnerability is that it is weakness. People were raised to believe that to be vulnerable and exposed is to be weak."

Brown argues that vulnerability is all about strength, about courage. I agree!

To paraphrase Ernest Hemingway, writing is easy: you just sit down at the typewriter and bleed.

These authors have owned their stories and are authentic in their storytelling, and for that I sing their praises. Each one has opened their heart and spilled a fraction of it on a page in exchange for you to understand how love transformed them, and in hopes that For the Love of Autism can transform you too.

WHAT LEGENDS ARE MADE OF

———

Tamika Lecheé Morales is a teacher, actress, author, speaker, entrepreneur, and president of The Autism Hero Project (AHP), a nonprofit organization after her own heart. This *"firessa"* does what she loves.

"As much as a mom raises a child, so does a child raise a mom."

HE IS LEGEND

I almost lost him, before I ever even had a chance to meet him. I was in my hospital bed so busy talking with family that I didn't even notice the beeping sound that grew louder and louder and more frequent. Then there was an ambush of nurses running into my room, my doctor right behind them. They asked my oldest son and in-laws to exit. A nurse was trying to put a disposable cover over my doctor's shoes as he hopped on one foot and then the other. My eyes widened, watching—yet I was unaware of the magnitude of what was happening.

That memory plays in SSSSLLLLLOOOOWWW motion. I recall vividly seeing and feeling their panic. The nurse pulled my blanket off. Both of us noticed that my water had broken. *Epidurals are some good shit, I thought, because I hadn't felt nada. Is this what all the hype was about? OK, damn, I know you asked me to tell you if my water broke but sorry, I didn't feel it.* Then I heard my doctor say, "We need you to start pushing now," and telling the nurse to have the suction ready. They kept looking at the machines hooked up to me. I followed their gaze and I finally realized—the beeping sounds were coming from me.

I studied the machine. Then I saw it. Saw the line of his heartbeat. Realized what was at stake. Instantly, the beeps blared louder. Before I could react, the doctor said, "Come on, Tamika. Pppuuuussshhh!" And so I did. The doctor grabbed the suction to try to pull him out. I could feel that he was finally out of me, but I didn't hear a cry. *Cry, I am supposed to hear him CRY!* And then I heard it. I heard him!

Maximillian Eros was born blue, with his umbilical cord wrapped around his neck. He was six pounds and six ounces of perfection, and he fought to be in this world. Now, I fight side-by-side with him, for him, and through him to be seen, heard, and appreciated. He belongs in this world.

YOU ONLY GET SO MANY FIRSTS; EACH ONE IS A BLESSING

My first true love, Sebastian, was born nearly sixteen years before Maxim. Sebastian and I experienced so many firsts together. I never thought I could love anything as much as I loved him. I was still growing up and discovering so much about myself. I laugh as I write this line because I still feel like this twenty-seven years later. With two siblings that far apart, everyone thought that Maxim was an "oops baby," but he wasn't. Sebastian was born one month after I turned twenty. Technically, Sebastian was an April Fool's joke I told his dad that wound up being true, and ten days later the joke was on me. I was in complete shock. He was meant to be. Sebastian was the first to teach me that as much as a mom raises a child, so does a child raise a mom. So, when Maximillian came along, I thought for sure that everything I did wrong the first time around with Sebastian I would remedy with him.

But parenting is hard shit.

It's beautiful and rewarding but hard, nonetheless. The constant second-guessing, the guilt, the sacrifices, all of it. You just pray that you don't go fucking them up and cause childhood trauma. I know some parents out there that make parenting look so damn easy. I am not one of those parents. But to be honest, I didn't have typical role models. I never met my father and, truth be told, he never knew of my existence. And from the age of nine until I graduated high school, I didn't grow up with my mother either. It was complicated. My brother and I left my mom and little sister one summer vacation to never return and instead my *abuela (Mami)* was the one to raise us. At the time, my mom lived in San Francisco with my sister and my sister's dad while we were in New York with my grandmother, uncle, aunt, and her six kids. Eleven of us— and sometimes more—lived in a two-bedroom apartment in the projects of Coney Island. We learned about struggle and persevering against all odds.

It wasn't until I became a mother that I realized how much I mourned growing up without a dad. Because of this, I count my blessings every day that I married a good man and that my boys have a strong father figure. Hugo is one-of-a-kind to be able to weather my "crazy" for nearly thirty years, because I am the first to admit that being my partner is arduous at times. I am the result of my circumstances. My dysfunctional upbringing inspired my first play, "The Nuyorican." Despite how hard life was then, we weren't poor—we just didn't have any money. But we were rich in know-how. I learned how to be loud when I needed to be heard. I learned how to advocate for myself when I didn't want to sleep on the big round chair or on the floor. I learned how to argue to get a sliver of *Mami's* king-size bed where four or five of us slept on any given night, and I learned how to fight when I needed to defend myself. Life was preparing me for what was to come, and this hindsight helps me to never regret my circumstances.

HE IS LOVE

My love for Maximilian is one of a kind. His innocence is angelic, and his love is pure. His love breathes life into me. I love him with every fiber of my being, and he makes it so easy to love him. He is funny, kind, smart, caring, and intuitive.

So, when I witness the stares, the rejection, and people's ignorance, it hurts. One example is Maxim's use of echolalia (noises and phrases on repeat). It's his form of stimming (self-stimulating or soothing behavior) and he does it loud and proud and a lot. He doesn't care where he is. It could be in class, at a restaurant, or—for some reason—in a quiet car ride whenever I suddenly need to take a phone call. He is unapologetic about it. Yet, as he grows older, I see the implications of growing up in an unaware and unaccepting world. People constantly judge what they do not understand and the compounding stares, bullying, unkind experiences, lack of grace, and misunderstanding in non-inclusive spaces and systems are subtly changing him. His joyous and effervescent ways, his very essence, are being stifled. I am slowly seeing the changes. Changing who he is. Changing the parts of him that should not have to change. Sometimes, change can be good, but some changes I am witnessing are a result of unacceptance. One new development is that he is exhibiting anxiety. This saddens me because I see all the good in him others stuck on "typical" fail to see.

THE LEGENDARY KID

Over time, I have also seen Maximilian step into his own identity. One day in third grade, I had been calling out to him repeatedly and he wouldn't respond. "Maxim… Maxim…Maximillian Eros Morales! Do you not hear me calling you?" Finally, I walked over to him and asked him what was up. With a completely straight face, he responded with, "That's not my name anymore." He was declaring a name change. He wanted now to be referred to as "The Legendary Kid." I found this so amusing—I entertained it. I loved it! I loved that he was advocating for himself even if he probably meant it as a joke initially. I quickly negotiated, explaining that "The Legendary Kid" was longer than his first name. Finally, we settled on "Legend." That same evening, I messaged his teacher that going forward please start calling him Legend at school. It's been years and now EVERYONE calls him Legend, including his grandparents.

A LEGEND IN THE MAKING: LIFE SKILLS 101

I've always encouraged Legend to be himself, to do what he loves, and to dare to try new things. We are a bilingual family, and I am a dual language teacher. Because I knew the benefits of a dual-language education, I didn't let Legend being autistic stop him from entering the dual-language program. It has been rewarding to see him become bilingual, biliterate, and bicultural. Since we live in the United States of America, it's no surprise that Legend has learned to favor English even though his first language was Spanish. To say that the level of Spanish and workload at the middle school level have come without challenges would be a lie. I'm not sure that Legend is up to the challenge much longer, but for now we stay committed until he knows for sure.

It could be cultural but often I witness moms do everything for their children, even the simplest acts. If their child finishes eating and walks away from the table, they pick up the dirty dish and wash it for them. If the child steps out of the bathroom after a shower, the parent picks up their dirty clothes and puts them in the hamper. They fold their laundry, pick out their clothes, pick up the messes of toys they leave behind. Even if their child is old enough, they toast their bread for them and make their snacks. They don't let their children do these things independently and that spills over into other areas of their lives. I too was guilty of this for a long time, but I started to think about Legend's future. He needed to learn important life skills. That's when I started thinking more intentionally. Granted, the child should be developmentally ready to take on these tasks, but you will never know if they are until you consistently try.

Legend is great at a lot of things, but his attention deficit hyperactivity disorder (ADHD) coupled with his autism means we have to constantly redirect his focus. We work hard to keep him on task. We work on things like reminding him to clean up after himself or washing out his lunchbox every day–his non-preferred tasks. These are chores that he is responsible for and we are waiting for the day that accomplishing these tasks will become intrinsic for him. Recently, we've started giving him an allowance so that we can incentivize him and teach him the value of work, earning money, saving, and spending.

Legend has a lot of GRIT. It's no wonder who he gets it from. While vacationing in Hawaii, he ventured into ziplining at great heights and over reservoirs by himself at the age of 8. He was a little nervous but asked to go alone after doing the first few ziplines attached to one of us. He loved it! So, when we returned to Hawaii two years later, he was completely down to try bike ziplining over the reservoir alone. I can't explain the sense of pride I had when he dared to rappel thirty feet off the platform by himself instead of taking the stairs. I knew he was a little scared, but he decided to go for it. I myself had butterflies in my stomach and needed to take a few breaths before I could take the plunge, but Legend ran off the platform without a second look and grinned with glory when he touched the ground! This is the same kid who had cried the day before about jumping into deep water and refused to do it even while his dad was in the water ready to catch him. I offered to hold his hand and jump with him, but he wasn't having any part of it. That day he just didn't want to, and I get it. Some days are just like this. Sometimes, I have to check in to make sure that I am not pressuring him and that he's doing something that he really wants to do for himself and not just to please us. I want him to experience doing things that he might find fearful so that he sees that he can overcome his fears. But in teaching him this lesson I have to make sure that it isn't going to emotionally scar him. I fight for this balance with both of my children. This is why we talk through things, though I recognize that this is a privilege other parents may not have.

Legend loves the spotlight and a video camera. He has been begging for his own YouTube channel, so I love to turn the camera on him and have him improv. He has great presence and is truly a natural. It's fun to watch him and I can't help but feel amused every time. I also look at it as him practicing public speaking skills, which even neurotypicals are fearful of doing. One year, we sponsored an Autism's Got Talent and Resource Fair through The

Autism Hero Project, and I wanted to do a mommy-and-son dance to Kelly Clarkson's song, "Broken and Beautiful." We only practiced a few times because I was so consumed with all of the details and organization of the event itself. Personally, I felt a little unprepared. I never got a chance to choreograph a small section in the middle of the song, and instead decided to do whatever came to me at that moment. But that kid went on stage and didn't skip a beat! He was fantastic and we got a standing ovation! The choreography was touching and emotionally provoking. Many parents cried. Maxim loves to remind me of the memory and always asks, "When are we doing the next Autism's Got Talent Show?"

NOT ALL HEROES WEAR CAPES

Legend is just one example of autism. Although he is showing success in some areas, I assure you that it came on the back of repeated attempts and never-ending practice. It took work. Attempts disguised as failure proved to be lessons on resilience and perseverance. There have been countless hours of therapy, starting with early intervention: developmental (DT), speech (ST), occupational (OT), food, equestrian, and Applied Behavior Analysis (ABA). We had no time for extracurricular activities because we were doing therapies five to six days a week and school full time. As he began graduating from one therapy, we added swimming, then karate.

Progress took time—actually, it took years. And progress is what we celebrate. I love that we are now working on other life skills in OT. He graduated from clipping fingernails and now is working on following recipes and making meals. When he was younger, we saw him make the most strides with ABA therapy. I know that there is controversy surrounding ABA, so I am only going to share our testimony. Legend learned to speak in full sentences and have a conversation. He learned to tie his shoes, button and zip up his clothes, memorize his address and phone number, look both ways before crossing the street, ride his bike, take turns while playing games, and we eventually got him to eat fruits and vegetables without crying and screaming bloody murder... Yo, you have no idea... these were game changers for us. Legend loved his therapists, and they became family.

Unfortunately, some employer-funded medical insurance policies and Medicaid in Illinois do not give children access to ABA therapy. Seeing what therapy did for Legend, I found it discriminatory that parents couldn't access life-changing therapy because of financial constraints. We were blessed to have insurance that covered ABA, even if we paid thousands of dollars out of pocket every year to meet the deductible and copayments. I wanted families to have access to all therapies that helped children unlock their full potential—including ABA—in hopes that they could experience the same success. Because of this, Legend became the genesis behind The Autism Hero Project (AHP), a 501c3 nonprofit organization.

AHP's vision is to "prepare kids with autism for the world and prepare the world for them." Our mission is to fund medical insurance for children to access the therapies they need to unlock their full potential. We also work to make inclusive spaces and have businesses and organizations make appropriate accommodations. We know that legislation is integral in creating a world that is inclusive for ALL, so we have been building relationships with lawmakers. One of our biggest accomplishments is the Illinois bill that I worked on with State Representative Barbara Hernandez to continue to raise awareness and gain acceptance for our community. Illinois House Bill 1954 was endorsed by State Senator Karina Villa and signed into law on August 27, 2021, by Illinois Governor J.B. Pritzker:

"The first full week of April of each year is now designated as Autism Acceptance Week to be observed throughout the state of Illinois as a week to promote awareness and acceptance of autism and to encourage school districts, organizations, businesses, and local residents to support this week and participate in informed educational events planned to commemorate the occasion." – Illinois Public Act 102-0588

This organization has become my life's work, and I am so proud of how far we've come. We soon sponsored nearly $200,000 in medical insurance for kids who otherwise would not have access, and that's all through grassroots efforts by a board and volunteers who are intentional about making a difference in our community. When people ask me to tell them about the work that we do I simply say, "Imagine having a need for your child that you couldn't provide. Then a group of HEROES come alongside you and says, 'We got you!'" AHP is that village of superheroes.

CONFESSIONS

The late President Franklin D. Roosevelt and others have said, "Bravery is not the absence of fear, but the action in the face of fear." We can't help being fearful. It's natural. A lot of my first fears that struck me instantly when I heard autism spectrum disorder (ASD) still exist today. I fear what I do not know, what I can't control, and I fear what's to come … the inevitable … death. My death, and what that means for him. I had hoped that in the same way that Legend has made me the best version of myself, Sebastian also would "level up." That he would want to be his brother's keeper. But he is not there yet. I know that it's unfair of me to expect him to take on such a responsibility. But the truth is, I do. And if he ultimately decides not to, I would judge myself for it. And without him meaning to, it would serve as another reminder of how I failed as a mom. If I can't make his own brother accommodate him, why should I expect the world to? So, I continue to forge ahead with determination for him to be seen and appreciated and I pray to never give up.

I also must confess that I get tired. I have devoted the last five years to growing AHP and it has literally become like a third child. I have seen the fruit of my labor in the countless testimonies that we have received and every day I am thankful to my board of directors. Specifically, my vice president Jaime Clark for running this organization with me. But I need to remind myself that AHP isn't a child. I have a child, his name is Legend, and he needs me, too. I dedicate so much of my time and energy daily to care for so many others that I leave my own family and myself for last. I struggle a lot with this, and I find solace in that AHP will reach a point where we can bring on more people and I can loosen the reins slowly but surely. In the meantime, I have to keep reminding myself that life is short, and I need to focus on what matters most, so I don't have a lifetime of regrets. Legend deserves this and I deserve him.

I know that within our autism community there is a great divide. There are arguments about representation, what colors to use, what symbols not to use, how to identify, what language to use, what organizations to boycott, which therapies to avoid, and who has the right to tell autism stories. Maybe we don't get it right all the time, but we can't continue to fight each other and slow down progress. Here are the facts—autism doesn't only affect the child, and we all have our own personal experiences, struggles and pain. There's not just one story that needs to be told. We all experience beauty, joy, grit, and hope. So, I encourage you to share your stories so that we can learn from one another, discover resources, find our voice, and activate others. Life is a one-time offer. Don't waste it dwelling on the deficits. Instead, ACT! And together, let's unite and make the world right for the love of autism.

Resources
- The Autism Hero Project (AHP) - autismheroproject.org
- Early intervention/therapies.
- Create your village, if you don't have one. Be proactive and start by being the village for someone else.
- Social media, follow pages like The Autism Hero Project, every author in this book, Fidget and Fries, Disability Scoop, and local support groups in your area.
- Listen to podcasts, including Adventures in Autism, Adulting on the Spectrum, and Welcome to our Table.

Hashtags
#ForTheLoveOfAutism #TheLegendaryKid #HeisLegend

My Love Letter
to The Legendary Kid

Dear Legend,

There is so much I want to say and yet, my words fail me. I wish I had the right words to convey all that you mean to me. I am a better human because of you. I love you with everything, and yet, I feel so unworthy of you.

You inspire me. You are amazing. You touch my soul and make me want to change the world so that you can be seen, heard, and appreciated. You make the world better, and I know it. I have centered my work on helping the world to know it too. This has become a colossal undertaking, and I can't do it alone. That is why I work like:

I'm running out of time
I write day and night, like I'm running out of time
Every day I fight, like I'm running out of time

Like tomorrow won't arrive
Like you need it to survive
I am not throwin' away my shot[1]

And when I don't have the spoons to keep digging, I look to you.

---

[1] Lin-Manuel Miranda, verses modified from "Non-Stop," Hamilton (2015).

But I know that I must ask for your forgiveness because in my race to change the world, I have failed to be present for you. For that, I am sorry, Legend. So, this letter will serve as my reminder to put you first. You deserve that.

I pray that you come to know a world that includes you.

You really are LEGENDARY, kid. You changed me. Your name was divinely inspired, and I can't wait to see the legend you'll become. And no matter what, Papi, Bastian, and I love you more than you can ever imagine.

With all my love and adoration,

Me

Photo Credit: Daisy Jimenez

TIPS FOR PARENTING CHILDREN WITH AUTISM

Dr. Temple Grandin is a renowned professor of animal science, livestock handling facilities designer, public speaker, and author on animal behavior and autism. She was named in CEOWorld Magazine's 10 Best Professors in the United States and *Time* Magazine's 100 Most Influential People in the World and has been inducted into the Women's Hall of Fame.

"Autism is an important part of who I am but having an interesting career has given me a fulfilling life."

One of the biggest mistakes some parents make when parenting a child with autism is to get locked into the label and fail to see the whole child. Debra Moore, my co-author of the book, *Navigating Autism*, introduced the term "label locking." Too often the child becomes the label. One of the problems with autism is that it ranges from a brilliant computer scientist to somebody who never learns to dress themselves. In its mildest forms, autism can be a variation in personality. When children with autism are ages two to four, the ones who will learn to talk and the ones who will always remain non-verbal may look the same. This is why early education is so important.

When I was two-and-a-half years old, I had no speech, and I was fortunate to enter an excellent early speech therapy program. There was a strong emphasis on learning how to wait and take turns, good life skills that parents should teach to their child. Many different activities can be changed into a turn-taking game. For example, if the child is spinning the wheel on a toy car, you can turn this into a turn-taking game by passing the car back and forth and taking turns spinning the wheel. The next step is for the child to learn turn-taking by playing simple board games.

When working with young children, it also is important to slow down when you talk. When my mother talked fast, her speech turned into gibberish. The third thing that parents and teachers need to do is to wait and give the child time to answer. The brain of autistic children is like a slow computer: it takes time to respond. If you push the child too hard, they are likely to "freeze" and not respond.

START EARLY EDUCATION IMMEDIATELY

Doing nothing is the worst thing parents can do if they have two or three year olds who are not talking. If services are unavailable, find some volunteers to come in and work with your child. Young autistic children need ten to twenty hours of one-to-one instruction per week. Parents ask me all the time: How can you determine whether or not you have an effective teacher? A young child is progressing if they develop more speech, become better at taking turns, and gain more skills such as washing their hands. These are all indicators of effective teachers. I remember some of my speech therapy classes, and I liked going to "talking school." If a child resists going to therapy, then something is wrong. If the child hates therapy, it is possible that the teacher is forcing them into sensory overload. Sensory oversensitivity is often a problem in autistic children and adults. There is more information on sensory problems on my website, templegrandin.com, and in my book, *The Way I See It.*

LIMIT VIDEO GAME TIMES

A big problem many kids with autism face is getting addicted to video games and doing nothing else. They need to get outside and play and interact with other children. Some people may criticize me for having old-fashioned views. However, I am not observing good results when the kids grow up. In fully verbal children with autism, I am seeing two adult outcomes. One young adult gets out and has a job and a life, and the other adult remains at home playing video games. Video games need to be replaced with other activities, such as playing games outside, crafting projects, and building Legos. When I was in third grade, I was using real tools to make real things. Childhood activities, such as scouting, hiking, collecting rocks, and making and flying kites, are great for children with autism.

In addition, too many kids today are afraid of making mistakes. They fail to learn important lessons from correcting their mistakes. This may be partly due to not doing enough hands-on activities. When I did hands-on activities, such as making kites, I learned to tinker and make changes in the design if my kite did not fly right. One of the biggest mistakes some schools have made is taking out the hands-on classes. Having classes in art, sewing, and woodworking helped make my elementary years successful, and it could help other children, too.

DON'T OVERPROTECT KIDS

Another big problem I am seeing today is that a child with a label, such as autism, gets overprotected and fails to learn new things. When I was seven and eight years old,

I would go into a store and buy stuff. Too many fully verbal teenagers are so overprotected that they have never gone shopping by themselves. I have talked to many moms, who explained to me that they had a hard time letting go. Several mothers have told me that when they gradually started letting go, they saw their child blossom, get a first successful job, or build independence.

My family did three things which helped me to develop during my elementary school years. They used teachable moments, instructed me on how to save money, and made me a hostess at parties to learn social skills.

1. **Teachable moments.** Autistic children do not instinctively learn social skills. They have to be taught. It is like teaching somebody how to behave in a foreign country. At the dinner table, there were many teachable moments. If I picked up the rice or green beans with my hands, mother would say, "Use the fork." She never yelled, "No." Instead, she would give the instruction and then tell me why I should use the fork. She would explain to me that other people thought it was disgusting when I ate with my hands. Each meal may have had two or three teachable moments.

2. **Learning about money.** When I was about seven years old, I got a small allowance that I could use to buy things. If I did chores around the house,

I could earn additional allowance. There were certain items that mother never bought for me, such as candy and little balsa wood airplanes. Those were designated as allowance items. I learned at a young age that if I wanted the more expensive plane with the propeller, I had to save for two weeks. Money was no longer abstract when I could see how differing amounts of money could buy different things.

3. **Party hostess and hosts.** All the kids in my neighborhood, when they were in elementary school, served as hosts and hostesses when their parents had parties. For these parties, I had to put on my best clothes, greet every guest, and serve the snacks. This taught social skills, such as shaking hands and learning how to talk to people. There are many opportunities for teachable moments during different activities, such as shopping or walking in a park. The key is to build them into the everyday of your child's life.

FRIENDSHIPS THROUGH SHARED INTERESTS

In elementary school, I was not bullied because my third-grade teacher explained to the other children that I had a disability that was not visible, such as being in a wheelchair. However, in high school, I did not fit in, and

I got thrown out of a regular high school after I threw a book at a girl, who bullied me. I then went to a special school for kids with autism or emotional problems, but I was still bullied. The only place where I was not bullied is where I had friends who had the same shared interests in horseback riding, electronics, and model rockets. The best way for an autistic child to make friends is to do activities, such as music, art, theater, robotics, or working with animals, where they can have friends through shared interests.

LEARN HOW TO WORK

There are many kids with autism who develop good academic skills, but lack both life skills and work skills. Doing chores in elementary school was the first step to learning working skills. Other activities that helped me to learn working skills when I was still in elementary school were selling candy for charity and running a drink stand. When my younger sister and I ran a drink stand on the front lawn of our house, we learned that you have to have sufficient supplies. I will never forget when we ran out of sugar. The drinks tasted terrible!

Older elementary school children and teenagers need to learn work skills by doing a scheduled task where somebody outside the family is the boss. Volunteer jobs at a church or a community center should start at age ten or eleven. The child has to learn what a job is and that they have to be on time and do what they are told. When I was thirteen years old, my mother set up a sewing job for me in the home of a seamstress, who did dress alterations. I really liked getting paid and I was a hard worker. At age fifteen, I cleaned nine horse stalls every day and fed the horses. One of the biggest problems I see today is high-school age autistic kids are not learning working skills. In contrast, the most successful kids will usually have two or three real jobs before they graduate from college. To help kids get jobs, parents should look for "back doors," such as a friend who owns a store or a contact through social media. It is important to find a job where your child can be successful. Avoid jobs with high multitasking, such as a busy take-out window. Quieter shops, such as an ice cream parlor, office supply store, or the bagging section at a grocery are more likely to be successful.

DEVELOP ENTREPRENEURIAL SKILLS

I also learned when I was a teenager to sell my work instead of selling myself. In high school, I started painting signs, and the first sign I sold was for a hair salon. I had to make a sign that a hair salon would like, so I decorated it with a portrait of the Breck Lady. (Breck was a major shampoo brand when I was a teenager.) I learned that the best way to sell my sign painting skills was to show people photos of the signs I had made: my portfolio. The portfolio contained my best signs. In college, I continued to paint signs for different business and college activities. When I started designing cattle-handling facilities, I used this same portfolio approach. When people saw my drawings and photos from previous projects, they were impressed. At many autism meetings, I have talked to parents about making a portfolio of their child's artwork, photography, or computer programming. Many said that it was a good idea, but previously they had never thought about it. Today, it is even easier to collect a portfolio. Simple websites can showcase a person's work. The portfolio also needs to be on a phone, so it will be instantly available to show to somebody that may be interested.

OPEN DOORS TO OPPORTUNITY

The entrepreneurial skills I learned as a child and in high school helped me get my career started in the cattle industry. I had an intuitive ability to see doors to opportunity. There is a scene in the HBO movie, Temple Grandin, when I go up to the editor of the *Arizona Farmer Ranchman* and I get his card. This scene is really important and it actually happened! I knew if I wrote for this magazine that it would really help my business. All the social training I had at my parents' dinner parties enabled me to have the courage to ask for his card. Within a week, I had written an article that summarized my master's thesis on the behavior of cattle in different types of squeeze chutes, and they published it. Within a few months, I became the livestock editor. I was able to see this "back door" to start my career, and both parents and children can find these paths to do the same.

FIGHT ANXIETY

By the time I was thirty-three years old, I had successfully completed several large livestock system design projects. However, throughout my twenties, I had increasing issues with panic attacks, anxiety, and constant colitis. My symptoms were very similar to descriptions of autistic "burnout" that I have read online. I was desperate. Nothing seemed to relieve it until I used a low dose of an old-fashioned antidepressant medication, desipramine. The constant panic attacks stopped, and the medication turned my life around. I have been on a low dose of desipramine from 1980 to the present. Since I have been on the medication, I have done some of my best professional work. My nervous system no longer revs at 200 miles per hour, and I am no longer in a constant state of fear. Often, too many medications are given to young children. However, some teenagers and adults can benefit from careful, conservative use of medication. Try one medication at a time to see if it works. The right medication should have an obvious beneficial effect.

MAKE PROGRESS: THE HBO MOVIE AND REPRESENTATION

About twenty years ago, I was approached by Emily Gerson Saines, a mother of a young adult, who is non-verbal. Emily runs an agency for actors in New York, and she wanted to tell my story. It took her ten years to find the right team of people to make the movie: Actress Claire Danes, Director Mick Jackson, and Writer Christopher Monger. The movie, *Temple Grandin*, aired in 2010, and I loved how the movie showed my visual thinking; in the film, my major projects were all replicated. Danes became me after she spent hours listening and watching old videos of my interviews and lectures. Some people have said that an autistic person should have starred in the movie. Twenty years ago, when this project started, this was on nobody's radar, including mine. If another movie was going to be made, I would include a more diverse cast with the lead played by an autistic person. Since the production of the movie, there is now much greater awareness of the importance of being more inclusive. This is a good step, and we can take it farther in how we speak and act. In this way, we can continue to advocate for ourselves or for children.

WHERE DO WE START?

At this point, I want to emphasize that autistic people can have many different talents. Some have mathematical-visual-spatial minds and may excel in math and computer programming. Others, like me, are object visualizers and we are good at art, mechanics, and understanding animal behavior. A third type thinks in words, and they may have extensive knowledge of their favorite subject, such as cars or history. Parents and teachers need to take the things their child is good at and expand them. Good teachers need to help autistic children and adults develop their strengths. The emphasis needs to move away from fixing deficits and toward enhancing the child's ability where they can excel in life.

Autism is an important part of who I am but having an interesting career has given me a fulfilling life. Children and teenagers need exposure to many different things so they can develop interests that can develop into careers. One reason I went into the cattle industry was that I was exposed to it when I was a teenager. Being autistic helped me in my work with animals because I am an extreme visual thinker and animals live in a visual world, not a verbal world. (This is described much more completely in my books, *Thinking in Pictures and Animals in Translation*.) If we focus on children's strengths, that builds them up. We can avoid label locking, unlock their capabilities, and set them up for success.

Resources

- *The Way I See It:* a comprehensive guide for parents and teachers who work with young children.
- *Navigating Autism: 9 Mindsets for Helping Kids on the Spectrum* (co-authored with Debra Moore): a book with nine strength-focused strategies for anyone working with children and teens on the spectrum.
- *Thinking in Pictures (My Life with Autism):* Dr. Grandin's autobiography, recommended for individuals experiencing anxiety.
- "The World Needs All Kinds of Minds, a TED Talk: www.ted.com/talks/temple_grandin_the_world_needs_all_kinds_of_minds

Website
templegrandin.com

Hashtag
#SeeTheWholeChild

My Love Letter to My Mother and My Mentors

Dear Mother, Teachers, and Mentors,

I want to thank my mother and all the teachers and mentors who helped me to live a full life and do lots of intellectually challenging work. They "stretched" me to try new things, but they were careful not to force me into overwhelming situations. Mother and my speech teacher got me talking and learning at an early age. My mother also helped me to develop my strengths in art. When I kept drawing the same horse head over and over, she encouraged me to draw the entire horse. She greatly broadened my artistic ability, and I thank her for this.

Another person I need to thank is my third-grade teacher. When I was eight years old, I was unable to read, and she helped my mother teach me to read with phonics. Mother taught me every afternoon after school, and within one semester, I went from no reading to sixth-grade level reading. I became a lover of books and reading.

I also want to thank the two mentors who helped me get through my teenage years: Ann Brecheen at her Arizona ranch and Bill Carlock, my high school science teacher. They both challenged me with interesting projects, and I continued to see them throughout my college years. Both mentors spent hours and days with me during the most difficult time of my life. Mr. Carlock got me interested and motivated to study by showing me that study was the pathway to becoming a scientist. Another important mentor was Jim Uhl, a former Marine Corps captain who was starting a small construction company. He sought me out to design cattle handling facilities. He was also extremely helpful in getting my business started designing equipment. All of these mentors were essential in helping me to launch a successful career as a university professor and innovator in the cattle industry.

All children need to have mentors who can help them grow into successful adults. My wish is that other children have these supportive mentors. I hope their teachers and parents guide them so they can find their strengths.

Sincerely,

Dr. Temple Grandin

BIOGRAPHY

Temple Grandin is a professor in the Department of Animal Sciences at Colorado State University. At age three, she was non-verbal and had all the symptoms of severe autism. Livestock handling systems designed by Dr. Grandin are used all over the world. Half the cattle in the United States and Canada are handled in a center track restrainer system that she designed for meat plants. She also developed an objective scoring system for assessing animal welfare during handling of cattle and pigs.

In 2010, *Time* magazine named her one of the 100 Most Influential People in the World and she also was featured in an HBO movie, *Temple Grandin*, starring Claire Danes. Articles about Dr. Grandin have appeared in the New York Times, Discover Magazine, Forbes, and USA Today. She also has appeared on shows, such as Larry King Live, 20/20, 60 Minutes, Fox and Friends, and has given TED Talks.

Her book, *Animals in Translation*, was a New York Times bestseller. Other popular books are: *Thinking in Pictures, Emergence Labeled Autistic, Animals Make Us Human, The Way I See It, and The Autistic Brain*. Dr. Temple has been inducted into the Women's Hall of Fame and the American Academy of Arts and Sciences. She has received numerous industry awards, including CEOWorld Magazine's Top 10 College Professors in the United States.

Photo Credit: Alison Bert
Headshot Photo Credit: Rosalie Winard

AUTISM AND FEELINGS: A BALANCING ACT

Eileen Lamb is an author, photographer, podcast host, and founder of The Autism Cafe.

"What I want for parents of autistic children is for you to know that no matter how lonely you may feel right now, you are not alone."

Autism.

A label that says so much about a person, yet so little at the same time.

I remember the day autism officially became part of our life. I say officially because, at that point, I had unknowingly lived with autism for twenty-six years. It took my son's diagnosis for the pieces to fall into place.

On the day my son, Charlie, was diagnosed with autism, a few weeks shy of his second birthday, I experienced a wide range of emotions. I remember the emptiness as the doctor handed us an educational pamphlet about autism; bright colors, happy people, useless to anyone with Google. With the pamphlet, she handed us a more serious document: Charlie's official diagnosis. And that was it. We were on our own. That was when it started, the moment the walls closed in, the floor dropped away, every other cliche I'd rolled my eyes at happened to me.

Deep down, I'd known for a while that Charlie was almost surely autistic. But without that paper, it was just a thought, a guess. Without the official diagnosis, I lived in a world where Charlie was still technically "normal," where he was still on track to meet those milestones that we'd all become so worried about, where we thought he'd catch up. I was prepared to hear the diagnosis—but still, it hit hard. I had questions. So many questions. Questions no one had an answer for. Questions that didn't have answers. Will my sweet little boy ever be able to say his own name? Will he go to school or play soccer? Will Charlie ever become an independent adult?

At the same time, another part of me felt relief. Finally, there was an explanation for Charlie's struggles. Autism. I wasn't a bad mother after all. No illness was hurting him. Charlie was healthy. His brain was just wired differently.

There are tons of happy, fulfilled people with autism in the world—why can't one of them eventually be Charlie? The diagnosis gave us a framework to help get him there, a path to follow. We would walk that path with him, fueled by our hope that he was one of the fortunate ones.

POST-DIAGNOSIS LONELINESS

For months, I lived under a grey cloud. Charlie had been making very little progress in therapy, and my sadness about it enveloped me. I was grieving. Yes, grief. I had experienced a loss, but at the time, I didn't know it. No one had died, nor had a loved one left me or moved far away. I was grieving . . . dreams. I needed to grieve elements of this once-future life I imagined that wouldn't ever be. I felt so guilty. Ashamed for feeling this way. Guilty enough that I buried those feelings deep inside.

Autism is complex in ways that many do not grasp. I'm not grieving my son. I grieve the heated discussion about what the greatest band of all time is. I lament the naivety that led me to believe all moms get to hear their child call them "mommy." I grieve a life that should have been easier for him, and by extension, for us, his parents. But most of all, I grieve all the varied experiences that, after it's all said and done, add up to a fulfilled and enriching life— experiences Charlie won't have. I do not grieve my son. I grieve for him.

I felt like my feelings made people uncomfortable,

that they were a burden. It took time to get comfortable with the idea that I could grieve the dreams I had for my future, all while still loving my child with every fiber of my being. And I did. And I do. I love Charlie. All of him. I don't want to change his personality and squash his quirks. Still, I so desperately want him to be able to express the many parts of him that autism cruelly locked away deep inside.

I tried opening up to people, but I often came out of these interactions feeling even worse, feeling misunderstood. They'd say, "He's gonna be fine," or "Autism is his superpower," and "My nephew has autism, and speech and reading caught up by age six." The comments came from a place of sympathy and support, but they brought even more pain. Autism wasn't a superpower, not for Charlie. We had no idea if he'd ever be "fine," whatever that even means. And, while it was genuinely wonderful that their nephew was doing so well, we were continually experiencing the artificial optimism and carefully chosen language Charlie's doctors and therapists used when describing his future hopes.

CONNECTING WITH OTHER PARENTS: A NECESSITY

While I tried to keep up appearances, the inevitable happened—my mom-friends began drifting. We simply had less in common now that the paths our children were taking had diverged so much. Plus, I didn't have the time nor the energy to socialize. Charlie had become a handful in public, not following directions that kept him safe, running off in an instant when I let down my guard, and screaming. He screamed a lot. And loudly too. He had no interest in other children, either. Looking back, I wonder if I'd have been happier if I hadn't tried to keep up with activities he didn't enjoy for so long, simply out of fear of losing my sense of normal.

So, maybe it's not a surprise that people started to fizzle out of my life. I get it. I do. It was a lot. My mom-friends stopped reaching out, and so did I. It's almost as if we had some type of nonverbal understanding that this wasn't working. We weren't a match anymore.

Still, I wished more people had tried reaching out to me, though I understand the discomfort and not knowing what to say. I wish someone had stopped by with sushi and wine or simply texted more to chat. It was lonely. I didn't have friends who "got it." I needed someone who knew what it was like to have a life filled with therapy, augmentative and alternative communication devices, and intense, inconsolable tantrums. But I didn't have anyone like this.

So, I spent a lot of time alone, reflecting, wondering what being a good mother even looks like for a child like Charlie. In this loneliness, what I could do was write down my feelings. So, I did. I started writing, and it was therapeutic.

I was still missing that crucial piece, though. There was hardly anywhere that I saw my experience mirrored. Now that I was at least expressing my feelings, I wanted someone to share them with—someone who'd understand. So, I took my writing a step beyond where I was comfortable and shared it on social media. It was time to get out of my shell and see who else was out there with children like Charlie. I knew I couldn't possibly be alone.

UNHEALTHY EXPECTATIONS FOR AUTISM PARENTS

It's a human fault, the fear of expressing your feelings. Well, it does have its purpose, but most often, it's a destructive trait. So many of us fear our emotions. We're afraid we'll be misunderstood. Afraid we'll get hurt. Or criticized. Afraid of . . . fear. So, we take the safe road, lined with walls to keep out the world.

It's a vicious cycle—the more we keep our emotional experience hidden, from ourselves or others, the more that cycle of loneliness continues onward, reinforcing the idea that this technique works. Well, it does work. It keeps out a painful moment or two, but it cements loneliness and deep disconnection. Plus, we begin to believe that we're the only ones feeling this way. We may even think something is seriously wrong with us. So, in turn, we're even less likely to open up.

It's vulnerable to express a controversial sentiment,

but it's a necessary vulnerability. You'll never know if someone feels the way you do if nobody ever knows how you feel. This, in a nutshell, is what motivates me to share my writing about the journey we're on. The message to my readers is, succinctly, you are not alone. It's what I had needed to hear—and still do—and it's the truth.

The expectations placed on parents of autistic children are often unfair and unhealthy. We're expected to take it all with a smile, for fear of being labeled a martyr or a child-hater. We're expected to be satisfied, as is, with the profound disability with which our child is forced to live, like the inability to communicate their needs or keep themselves safe. All of this, in the name of autism acceptance.

Autism isn't a tragedy, but it isn't a gift for everyone. *This should be okay to say.* Many people with autism cannot use it to their advantage and experience heartbreaking setback after setback. It's a reality that many higher functioning autistics refuse to acknowledge, often leading to heated discussions on social media, between parents and autistics themselves.

THE SOCIAL MEDIA WAR: AUTISTICS VS. PARENTS

After I began to open up online, I found myself in a world I had no idea existed. I was thrown right into an online battlefield between so-called "autism moms" and self-identified "autistic advocates." I quickly learned that if you're the mother of an autistic child, expressing anything online but the utmost gratitude for your child's autism leaves you vulnerable to vicious attacks, threats, and harassment from the autistic community—bullying.

There is a distinction between autism itself and the autistic community. The autism community is everyone touched by autism, and the autistic community is primarily autistic adults with the capability to go online, read, talk, and opine. A core belief of this vocal group is that only autistic individuals should discuss their experience with autism because they're the ones with the diagnosis. As a parent interacting online, you might find yourself swarmed with comments that they know better than you, the parent, what your child needs and what they're experiencing, due solely to their shared diagnosis.

While that may be true on a small scale, it's mostly inaccurate. I'm autistic, but that doesn't mean I understand how your child experiences autism. A parent or guardian has that everyday detailed view—the autism spectrum is broad and no two autistic people have the same strengths and weaknesses nor the same array of autistic characteristics.

For instance—and I'm autistic and typing these words—I advocate for myself and my son. I struggle, but I get by. Of course, the best expert on an autistic person is, simply, that autistic person. The issue is that this cannot apply to the many people on the spectrum who can't communicate their needs and struggles, or perhaps much of anything at all.

In those cases, who better to advocate for this child, to interpret their behavior, than someone who observes and cares for them twenty-four seven? People on the severe side of the spectrum, like my son, will need some degree of twenty-four seven support for the rest of their life. Many autistics engage in behavior that makes it difficult to stay safe. Maybe they're aggressive towards themselves, maybe toward others. Autism is too broad for any autistic to speak for all other autistics.

An autistic person who can self-advocate on social media doesn't experience autism the same as someone with severe autism. Many autistics make it to adulthood without ever learning how to communicate. To use a toilet. Inspirational stories are great, but we can't forget about the autistic person who can't share their own story.

Recognizing that severe autism is a reality for many is not saying that high-functioning autism is easy. I know firsthand that it's not. But I'm also aware that advocating for myself is a privilege—a privilege offered to me by my ability to express feelings and ideas. I feel fortunate that my autism is not severe. For this, I like the analogy of someone who's visually impaired compared to a person who's legally blind. They have the same condition, but not to the same degree. Being able to see a little bit is a much different experience than seeing nothing at all. Sometimes it almost feels as if the many people who speak publicly about their higher-functioning level of autism feel threatened by severe autism. Like it belittles them and their experience. Acknowledging that severe autism exists would require admitting that their experience as high-functioning individuals doesn't give them insight into the mind of every autistic. And, therefore, it would be admitting that they are in no place to speak over and speak for the parents of severely autistic children.

Autistic people are not a singular entity. No one person or group can speak for all of us. I speak only for myself and, in some ways, for my son, and only until the point where he might be able to do it himself. As autistic special education professor, Dr. Stephen Shore, said, "If you know one person with autism, you know one person with autism."

We won't accomplish anything good by yelling on the internet. I'm sad to see a community that should be united and supportive often be so toxic and divided. I wish we could focus on the common ground we might have to improve life for autistic people and their caregivers.

One space that does this well is the Facebook group called, The "Autistic Community" Doesn't Speak for Me. It is my safe place. Parents aren't shamed for asking questions or feeling sad. There is no policing on terminology. Differences in opinions are welcome as long as it's respectful. I hope that these respectful conversations will become the norm and not an exception.

YOU ARE NOT ALONE

What I want for parents of autistic children to know is that no matter how lonely you may feel right now, you are not alone. It's common to feel isolated after an autism diagnosis enters your life. I spent quite a bit of time feeling that way. I know too well what it's like to feel that no one else gets it. Parents need community and these communities exist. The Facebook groups The "Autistic Community" Doesn't Speak for Me, as well as my own group, Autism—All Across the Spectrum, are two communities where you'll feel welcome instantly. Being a parent is complicated enough on its own, but raising an autistic child comes with its own set of struggles—we don't need or want constant judgment from strangers. We're doing the best we can to help our children while dealing with our feelings, too. And sometimes, we are too tired to try our best, and that's okay too. We're the first to be disappointed in ourselves when we fail. I hope you find relief in knowing that many of us are out here on this same journey. We are not alone.

Resources
- The Facebook group, The "Autistic Community" Doesn't Speak for Me. ABA therapy has been an amazing resource for my profoundly autistic child, Charlie. They taught him to communicate basic needs using an AAC device, and for that I'm forever grateful.

My Love Letter to Autism

Dear Autism,

You and I, we've been through a lot together. It took me a while to see you. It took me a while to realize how much control you had over me. It took me a while to realize that you were the reason I was called "different."

I like being different. I mean, sometimes I do. While growing up, it wasn't easy. Remember the other kids? As hard as I tried, they just didn't like us much. Maybe the quirks were too much or our interests were too "weird." I think volcanoes, mythical creatures, and music from the 1930s are all awesome. Maybe they were missing out!

I have to say, though, I do admire how you are unapologetically yourself. I like that about you. About us.

Forgive me for being blunt (that's your fault!) but I do wish, sometimes, you'd let go of me. Not forever and not in every way, but, you know. Just so I could experience going to the grocery store unafraid! And so, I could maintain a friendship. I've heard that people actually enjoy grocery shopping. Weirdos, I tell ya.

So, there's something that's been weighing on me. I want you to let go of Charlie. Let go of Charlie in all the ways that hurt him. In too many ways to count, you are holding my beautiful boy hostage. Charlie can't communicate because of you. In the spirit of honesty and openness I have goin' here, I think it's borderline abusive.

You gotta understand . . . Charlie has needs he desperately wants to communicate. Important things. He screams and cries—sometimes, he even hits himself from the sheer frustration of not being understood.

I'm sorry, I don't mean to be completely negative. It's not like that. Not exactly. I just know you so well. You're my oldest friend. So, let me thank you for something. Even though you make many styles of communication quite difficult for me to process, still, you allow me a voice. And for that, I know how grateful I am.

If there's any way you could keep it casual with Charlie like how you do with me, I—well, I know a boy who'd surely appreciate it. Next time you see him, maybe you can ask him what his favorite color is. Or if he loves sunsets like me. No, I know. I know you can't tell me. Maybe, though, the next time you're with Charlie, even though I do it every day, just to be absolutely sure he knows, if you would, tell him "Mommy loves you."

With love and no eye contact,
Eileen

BIOGRAPHY

Eileen Lamb, author of *All Across The Spectrum* and *Be The One,* is the founder of The Autism Cafe. She's also a writer, photographer, and host of the podcast, Adulting on the Spectrum. Born in France, Eileen now lives in Austin, Texas, with her husband and two sons, Charlie, nine, and Jude, six. On her blog, *The Autism Cafe*, she shares the ups and downs of raising a severely autistic child while being on the autism spectrum herself. In her free time, Eileen enjoys daydreaming and road trips.

Website: theautismcafe.com
Email: eileen@theautismcafe.com

Social Media
Instagram/Facebook/Twitter/Pinterest: theautismcafe
TikTok: eileen.lamb

Hashtags
#DearAutism #TheAutismCafe #YouAreNotAlone

MY JOURNEY FROM NONSPEAKING TO DOCTORATE IN EDUCATION

Dr. Kerry Magro, EdD, is an award-winning professional speaker and best-selling author, who is on the autism spectrum.

"Autism can't define me. I define autism."

"You have autism? You don't look like you have autism!"

If you'd told me I would receive comments like this when I was nonspeaking, I'm not sure if I would have believed you. Many people call my autism an "invisible disability," although I still deal with challenges people don't often see. My autistic journey started with my parents. Seeing early signs of autism, such as no speech and sensory processing challenges, encouraged my parents to go through the gauntlet to help me receive a formal diagnosis.

Expert after expert was consulted until Margaret Hertzig at Cornell Medical Hospital finally told my parents my formal diagnosis: Pervasive Developmental Disorder-Not Otherwise Specified, a form of autism. We as a society need to do a better job of making this process quicker but more cost-effective for families in poverty. Early intervention is the key.

Back then, in the early 1990s, experts didn't know much about autism. Because of the movie Rain Man, many people assumed that all autistic people were boys, great at math, socially awkward, and could win you a ton of money at the blackjack table. We also didn't have the benefit of the internet to research signs of autism. This is a reason, in my opinion, we are seeing such a significant increase in autism diagnoses today. More people are aware, so fewer individuals are falling through the cracks in terms of supports through this digital age.

But even so, back in those days (wow, that makes me feel old to say "back in those days"), I'm not sure anyone would have predicted that my life would be like this. That, years later, I'd be writing this, telling you that I graduated from college at Seton Hall University and continued my learning for a master's degree in strategic communications, also at Seton Hall. A few years later, I earned my Doctorate in Education from New Jersey City University.

I also doubt others would have predicted that I'd write several books that have reached an Amazon bestseller list for special needs parenting. They wouldn't have expected me to work as an autism entertainment consultant to bring a realistic portrayal of autism and other disabilities to our entertainment industry and to have a full-time job as a public speaker.

When I typically explain my journey, I start at the beginning, and it all begins with my . . .

EARLY CHALLENGES: NONSPEAKING

It wasn't always easy. Finding my voice took time as I was nonspeaking until I was two-and-a-half years old and didn't start speaking in complete sentences until seven years old. I began with occupational, physical, and speech therapy when I was diagnosed. Later, finding my voice would include music and theater therapy as those were two of my laser-focus key interests. I also was interested in basketball and fell in love with the sport at around eight years old.

When I share my experience with these therapies, many parents ask me what helped me build my communication. For me, technology was part of it. However, other factors, such as music and my parents mimicking any sounds I was making to nurture speech played a crucial role. Meeting your child where they are in their own development should become a mantra for all parents reading this.

These key interests became a massive part of helping me reach more and more developmental milestones and getting me ready for the career I have today. I performed in over twenty plays and was our team's high school basketball captain my senior year. Being on a team helped me build on my social skills while also having some close friends when making friends was still tricky due to my social challenges.

My challenges did not stop at friendships, though, as I was a victim of bullying. I was terribly shy and came off as the quirky kid, which made me an outcast. It wasn't until I was ten that I went to a school for kids with learning disabilities called Community Lower School in Teaneck, New Jersey. There I saw progress with these challenges. A big part of this was because every student knew they had something that made them who they were.

LEARNING THAT I WAS AUTISTIC

My journey would take a turn about one-and-a-half years later when I finally found out about my autism diagnosis in a social skills class. We were playing Disability Celebrity Bingo and learned that celebrities like Michael Jordan had ADD, Magic Johnson had ADHD, Leonardo DiCaprio had dyslexia, etc. At the end of the class, the teacher told us, "Some of the most talented people in the world are special . . . just like you."

When my teacher said this, I was confused. I raised

my hand and said, "So, why am I special?" My teacher told me I'd have to talk to my parents about that. Later that day, when I got home, I sat my parents down and asked them that same question. That was when they told me, "Kerry, you have something called autism. This means you learn a little differently, but it doesn't make you any less of a person."

I wouldn't realize it at that moment, but that was life changing. Years of knowing I was special but not knowing why I was special now made sense. It began my road to learning more about my strengths and challenges and advocating for myself. Shortly after that, I started sitting in on my Individualized Education Plan meetings to learn more.

TRANSITIONS

Middle school was ending, but Community Lower School also had a high school, Community High School. Many of the students from the lower school attended the high school, which helped me transition to secondary education without too many frustrations.

While things were looking good going into my freshman year, I was obese and dealing with some challenging behaviors due to puberty. One of the biggest challenges was going through a growth spurt and having back pain. Due to being introverted, I tended to let things build up around uncertain routine changes instead of talking to someone about it. I also wanted to start dating for the first time.

To get into better shape and make some friends, I tried out for our Junior Varsity (JV) basketball team as a point guard. A 230-pound point guard when most of the other freshmen trying out were 120 to 130 pounds. Needless to say, I didn't make the team, but I worked out five days a week that summer, lost sixty pounds, and made the JV team my sophomore year. I also made some incredible friends, and this turned me into my extroverted self. Many of my challenging behaviors deescalated because I could confide what was bothering me to a friend.

High school was pivotal for me in my academic career when I learned with educator Vincent Varrassi. He embraced what students "could do" while helping improve what they couldn't. It was refreshing when he'd ask me about my interests and met me at my level of learning. Another significant person was David Fisher, a world-renowned author who taught our English class every now and then. I remember a time when we were in class, all working on a short story. Seeing my enjoyment and seeing the story through to the finish inspired me to write more. I owe a part of my work today as an author to him.

Another area that helped me with my challenging behaviors was building self-motivation and doing well in my fundamental interests. When I was younger, my parents used reward systems (for example, a nice sticker a day when I did the desired behavior). I was thankful for my teachers pushing me towards my interests, so when I was in high school, I could rely less on rewards and wanted to succeed because it felt good.

The other puberty question that came up was relationships. As my high school journey came along, I had more feelings towards the opposite sex until I met someone who became my first-ever girlfriend. Ironically, she was the varsity cheerleader captain at the same time I was varsity basketball captain. I appreciated that in our relationship we had an open line of communication to avoid misunderstandings. Even to this day, I still have challenges with facial cues at times, so talking became an essential theme for each relationship I've had.

AFTER HIGH SCHOOL

As I accomplished more milestones, the possibility of college started to come to fruition. Experts' comments when I was a kid were, "Kids with Kerry's autism diagnosis are lucky to graduate from high school . . . let alone go to college." By the time my junior year of high school came, I knew that going to college was a strong possibility due to my good grades. However, I was unsure if my struggles with standardized testing would prevent me from getting into my top choices for schools, a common challenge for many members of our autism community. Despite having some of the best tutors, I got, in my opinion, mediocre SAT scores. For weeks after, I wondered if I was college material.

Knowing I was feeling this way, my parents encouraged and helped me apply to fifteen colleges. The goal was to just get in somewhere. Finally, at the beginning of senior year, my first letter came in from Seton Hall University while I was dealing with anxiety waiting for letters. It took days before we could open that letter to see the results, but once we did . . .

I found out I got in. My top choice. I was going to college. I was proving the experts wrong. Then the following fourteen letters came in, and I found out that I was accepted into all fifteen colleges.

In my freshman year of college, I disclosed my autism diagnosis to our Disability Support Center and was surprised to learn that I wasn't getting an Individualized Education Program (IEP) in college. Today as a full-time public speaker, I encourage schools to provide more services for teens with disabilities so they can prepare for the transition from IEP to the federal Section 504 for reasonable accommodations. Despite this new area that I had to learn about, I took it in stride as I became more comfortable being my own best advocate.

This didn't all come overnight. My parents became advocates to help me with this transition by encouraging me to find tutors and to be social. We didn't do much role playing—now, I recommend role playing to more parents if their autistic children have challenges with transitions and/ or anxiety. However, my parents and I did talk about tasks

I'd need to do to self-advocate. For example, my mom and dad were soundboards for me when it came to asking for accommodations like extended time on tests and a private room to take tests in.

This self-advocacy inspired me to realize that other students with disabilities might be going through similar challenges and be open about self-advocacy efforts to help our community. I came out to my peers about having autism during an oral communication class for the first time. This is where I penned a quote I have used to this day: "Autism can't define me. I define autism." For the most part, my peers were comforting and accepting, which made a world of difference. After completing my sports management degree from Seton Hall in four years, I decided to move to communications for my master's with a scholarship from the National Speakers Association to pursue a career in public speaking and continue to support our disability community.

This experience was quite different. Even though I was still at Seton Hall, there were far fewer students in each class. This helped me to establish a better rapport with each professor, which made for a more nurturing learning environment. In addition, the number of tests, which I dreaded during my undergraduate work, went away, replaced with papers and online assignments. A small challenge I dealt with was having some all-online courses. While I enjoyed not having to travel to class, it was more difficult to build rapport with my professors.

Two years later, after getting a higher GPA than during my undergraduate work, I graduated. After feeling I had accomplished all I could academically, I worked in digital marketing for four years for an autism nonprofit in New York while continuing my public speaking work. It was the self-advocates I met at this nonprofit, along with other members of our autism community, that lit a greater fire for my passion for disability advocacy. Because of that, I decided to start my Doctorate in Educational Technology Leadership at New Jersey City University in the hopes of one day becoming an adjunct professor.

My doctorate was completely online minus two weeks each summer for our cohort's in-person learning. At first, this led to challenges in building rapport, similar to my master's online classes. Thankfully, though, having a passion for technology at this point, I instantly bonded with most of my cohort via Google Hangouts. As I tell the autism families I work with, embracing technology can make a world of difference, no matter how old your child on the spectrum is. Three years later, I was officially Dr. Kerry Magro, EdD.

Along with writing, speaking, and consulting, I now live independently, am a nonprofit founder, have had my own car (driving was a challenge initially), have had seven girlfriends (I promise I had them one at a time!), and am living my definition of the best quality of life possible. I still deal with challenges due to my autism, such as having issues with routine changes, misunderstanding the perspectives of others at times, and finding friendships. Still, I have become an extrovert and am doing much better in these areas. In the future, I hope to get married and raise a family while continuing my work. I think I could make a good dad one day.

If I could leave you, the reader, with anything, it would be this: While autism is a spectrum, meaning that my journey may be vastly different compared to the next autistic person you meet, there's a lot of hope out there to help autistics live the best quality of life possible. We are learning more about autism every day. But, in this learning, I hope we don't forget those who are autistic and will need lifetime support.

I now say in my talks that "autism doesn't come with an instruction guide. It can sometimes come with a family who will never give up." Those self-advocates, parents, educators, family members, therapists, and other community members alike strive to make a better day for our community.

We are on our way!

Resource
- David Fisher, author, www.dfisher.com

My Love Letter to Autism

Hey, Autism!

We've certainly had an exciting ride.

When I was just diagnosed, there were times of uncertainty.

You see, autism, you've impacted me in a way that will always be slightly different than the next autistic. You are, of course, a spectrum. Sometimes we had challenges with communication and sensory issues, but today we are doing much better. Other times I was labeled as "different," which led to bullying, but I wanted you to know I found people in my life who accepted me for exactly who I am.

You have helped me to laser focus on my key interests of sports and theater, which has helped me turn some of those interests into a career.

And autism, you may not know this, but you've even become more well-known now than when I was a kid.

Dan Aykroyd once mentioned you and said that you, in part, made him successful as an actor.

Other celebrities, like Elon Musk, Wentworth Miller, Anthony Hopkins, Daryl Hannah, and Susan Boyle, also have mentioned they are autistic, too.

There are even people like Albert Einstein, Steve Jobs, and Mozart rumored to be autistic as well.

As we learn more about you, I'm excited for our society to try and find more ways to help autistics find more of the strengths it can bring while working with those who have additional needs and may need lifetime care.

A lot more people have you, autism, and I hope they can all succeed.

Sincerely, Kerry

BIOGRAPHY

Dr. Kerry Magro, EdD, is an award-winning professional speaker and best-selling author who is on the autism spectrum. Nonspeaking until two-and-a-half. Kerry travels the country to help others find their voice. In addition, Kerry is CEO and President of KFM Making a Difference, a nonprofit organization that hosts inclusion events and has provided college scholarships for students with autism. In his spare time, he hosts a Facebook Page called Kerry's Autism Journey that has about 215 thousand followers. There, he makes videos to highlight self-advocacy efforts. His videos have been watched over 35 million times.

Kerry's best-selling books *Defining Autism From The Heart*, *Autism and Falling in Love*, and *I Will Light It Up Blue!* have all reached Amazon Best Seller Lists for Special Needs Parenting. For his efforts, Kerry has been featured on NBC's Today Show, CBS News, Inside Edition, Upworthy, and HuffPost. Kerry resides in Hoboken, New Jersey. You also can invite him to speak with your school or business via email at Kerrymagro@gmail.com.

Website
KerryMagro.com

Social Media
Facebook fan page: KerrysAutismJourney
Facebook author page, Twitter, LinkedIn,
Instagram, TikTok: KerryMagro
YouTube: KerrysAutismJourney

Hashtag
#AutismCantDefineMe

DRIVING ON A SELF-DETERMINED ROUTE

Andrew Arboe is the Director of Community Outreach for Planning Across the Spectrum and the Founder of Driving with Autism. You can connect with him on autism, driving, transportation, and employment through email and LinkedIn.

"Strive for the next best thing and be accountable to yourself. Find your passion and never look back."

BLACK AND WHITE VS. GRAY MENTALITIES

Black-and-white thinking is a barrier to truly understanding the world. I strived to bring a gray perspective to life because I found that every person and every issue was full of nuance. I came to see black-and-white thinking as a barrier to truly understanding the world and I have seen the problems it can cause. I met with individuals in the autism community so concerned with blaming a specific thing for their difficulties that they became blind to the possibilities. They chose not to see the potential in self-improvement and seemed to end up attacking others instead of working to create a better life for themselves. This all created what I saw as an unending cycle of toxicity, one that I vowed to avoid. It is still one of the hardest things for me to overcome because of my own tendencies to think in black and white, but I work every day to keep nuance and the bigger picture in mind. I follow my own route and it has defined how I live my life. This same route has taken me to my current rewarding and fulfilling work in transportation.

THE REASON TO DRIVE

The biggest milestone I reached in my young adult life was undoubtedly learning how to drive. When I talk about driving in the context of autism, most people are surprised. In all the autism and special education conferences I attended in Connecticut from 2016 to 2018, most of the conversation around autism and transportation was focused on access to public transportation. I was using the bus system to get to my community college and a part-time job. I never considered driving at the time because it felt unnecessary. It was not until researching potential jobs where driving was required that I began to understand the possibilities that learning to drive could open. I was pursuing disability specialist jobs and I realized driving was a valuable skill, so I considered learning it. Upon researching how autistic individuals can pursue driving, I was surprised at the lack of resources in my state of Connecticut and the near complete absence of articles on the topic. The articles I found were convinced most autistic people could not follow that route, even after I discovered the statistic that one-third of autistic individuals with no intellectual disabilities have a license. While I knew that some autistic individuals who did drive, there was never a Temple Grandin of driving for me to have as a role model. I still felt like I was forging my own path in a community that had closed itself off to the bigger possibilities. But I knew there was a chance I could successfully learn to drive, and it was important to me, so I stuck to it.

I certainly love my father but practicing driving with him was a shaky experience. I cannot blame him for being so nervous since there was a lack of public awareness that many autistic people could successfully learn to drive. Nonetheless, I was constantly aware of my father's anxiety, and this only increased my own. I could feel the tension during our driving sessions, and I couldn't escape it. There were days where I would get by well and other days that were a struggle. At times, I was concerned that this might just not work out. Part of me wanted to blame my state and the schools for the lack of resources and for not doing enough to get people ready for driving. But I knew I had to stay focused on what I could do about it. That was when I decided to pursue driving as far as I could, despite my own fears and the difficulties posed by the state.

CREATING A ROUTE TO DRIVING

Knowing that pursuing driving was going to take me down an unknown route, I tried to make full use of the resources I had available. I used a typical driving school to obtain both education and on-road practice. It was nice being in an environment where I could focus on getting more comfortable while driving at my own pace. It really helped that the instructors were patient the entire time; it allowed me to get the basics down and showed me that I could successfully drive under the right conditions. I eventually completed driver's education and I had to figure out the next part of my journey on my own. The big problem was that I needed to practice but only had time to practice on the weekends. This limited my practice time, but I had to deal with it because I had no other options. My life was very busy, and I needed to be on a route that worked for me. At this stage, I focused on a few important things that led to gaining a lot of self-confidence in driving.

Those I want to highlight include:

1. **Use knowledge of the environment to your advantage.** Being knowledgeable about where you're currently driving and your destination can make the whole experience a lot more comfortable. If there is a place you drive to a lot, think about how that area works. How many lanes of traffic are there? How many traffic lights? Are there streetlights or is it dark at night? You can have someone else drive you around there a few times or you can use Google Maps to see the roads in the area beforehand. There's a lot of options when it comes to learning more about the environment you'll be driving in, so take advantage of them!

2. **Have a supportive team.** While my father was certainly anxious about the idea of me driving, he also was supportive. It meant a lot to me to be reminded that even after the difficulties I'd had, he still believed in me. I also had friends who were kind enough to help me ease into driving. One friend used cones to help me with parking, another friend was constant moral support, and a third friend took the time to show me the basics of parallel parking. This allowed me to get different perspectives on how people see my driving and reminded me that there were multiple people who believed in my success.

3. **Find reasons to drive.** When I started to drive, I had a list of places I really wanted to go but that I knew I would have to drive to get there. I used this motivation to remind myself of the good and exciting reasons to drive. I used places like conventions, conferences, restaurants, and other social outings to get more practice driving. I started going to as many things as I could find that seemed interesting, and anything at all related to my special interests. Some of my interests included visiting coffee shops, gaming, and going on hikes. Beyond things that excited me, though, I also focused on driving to develop specific skills. I have done specific drives, like when I drove through a rainstorm just to attend an autism conference that, coincidentally, introduced me to my current employer. I wanted to get better at driving in the rain, so I found a way to get in some practice. These skill-specific drives were eye-opening and really felt like I was taking on a new challenge head-on. I found ways to make myself want to drive, and because of that, I drove a lot more and got more practice than I ever expected.

4. **Have role models.** Having someone to admire can be self-inspiring. This goes beyond just people who believe in you to people who make you believe in yourself. There were some hard

days that made me question if learning to drive was really for me. During those periods, I thought back to my role model, a video game director named Yoko Taro. He directed the NieR series of complex and interesting games that are self-reflective and explore different themes about humanity. In an interview, Taro talked about how the game industry would tell him to go one way in developing games and he decided to go the opposite direction, just to see if there were other options. He didn't know what he would find in that direction, but he wanted to see it for himself. His games are now cult classics and getting more popular because of his unconventional style. I thought about that excerpt from the interview, and it always seemed to reaffirm that I must genuinely find out if driving was a possibility for me.

THE FATEFUL DAY: ROAD TEST

Then came the road test. The defining moment, was the moment when I could obtain a driver's license. After months of practice, I went to my Department of Motor Vehicles (DMV) on October 30, 2018. It felt urgent for me to pass the test on the first try because I was in the process of graduating from my community college. I was working as a job coach to help me graduate. But gaining long-term employment in my field was all I could think about. I really wanted something that connected with my coaching experience, and I knew a driver's license might be necessary for finding the right job. I sat at the DMV during the waiting period for this last challenge, anxiously working to keep my nerves in check by thinking of my role model's words and my ambitions for employment. In the end, I kept my cool, and remembered as much as I could from all my practices to the very end. Once I saw the "passed" tag on my evaluation, I was ecstatic.

FROM CHALLENGE TO SPECIAL INTEREST TO ACCIDENTAL WORK

I never intended for my work on driving to become a major part of my life's work. I mainly intended to present on the topic at some schools and autism organizations. I wanted to insert the idea into current conversations surrounding autism and transportation, in addition to other ideas that I found important to me. At my first presentation, thirty people attended, and when I threw my first workshop, three amazing organizations came to learn from me. One of them was a driving school that wanted to do more with the autism population, and they wanted to talk about working together to design an entire program for autistic drivers. It was a partnership that lasted nearly two years and one I learned so much from, too. Above all, though, I learned that my experience and perspective could really help a lot of people.

My employer, who allowed me to present on this topic, was impressed by the reactions and became my closest ally in my work. He told me that he never thought of transportation being a struggle for autistic people; it had just never occurred to him. Since then, he has routinely sent people to me to talk about driving and autism. I have a passion for what I do and the people who want me to do it, and that's extremely exciting. It's one of the major reasons why I've been able to work full-time since 2020. I spent a lot of time talking to parents and new drivers to help them develop strategies and ideas that they can use in their own learning-to-drive journeys. I've given webinars, spoken at conferences, and even written for the *Autism Spectrum News* on driving and other autism-related topics. This experience inspired me to become an entrepreneur and start my own business called, Driving with Autism, where I focus on driving prep education for individuals nationwide.

One of the best aspects of my work is that it is truly never-ending, because every time I go for a drive, I get something new out of it. When I first started driving, I found out that driving with video game music works great for me. Soundtracks from Nintendo, *Final Fantasy*, and the *NieR* series give me the most focus and basically put me in a state where I feel ready to drive. This was an unbelievably exciting revelation that changed driving for me forever. And every time I drive, I learn something new, and I get excited all over again.

CREATING YOUR ROUTE!

Deciding to drive and rejecting the expectations of my community stuck in their own ways defined my career and changed my life. It gave me a purpose in my life where I felt compelled to improve my abilities every day. If it wasn't for learning to drive, I would have not met my employer. I might have still been working part-time and only scratching the surface of the limitless opportunities and potential I have. My current position is being the director of community outreach with specific tasks that tackle driving. I consult with parents and new drivers in all fifty states and connect to organizations on the topic of driving. Now that I've seen what I can really do, all I want is for people to find their own sense of empowerment on their own terms. I would love to see more people create other non-driving transportation projects. I know that driving is not for everyone, and I am excited to see others with different passions channel theirs like I channeled mine.

Despite all the chaos in the world, there is room where people can really engage with their passions to create meaning and enrichment. I've seen it. I've lived it. Working on my passion for two years has been worth it. Strive for the next best thing and be accountable to yourself. Find your passion and never look back. Forge your path.

My Motivational Letter to Young Adults

Dear Young Adults,

Whatever happens in your life, you can forge your path. It is not going to be easy, but it can be done. Find your passion and be accountable to yourself to find enrichment. People and even groups will tell you that there is only one way, but there are more choices out there. Go the opposite direction and find for yourself if other options exist. You never know what you will find.

While we tend to place time limits on ourselves, it is never too late to improve your situation. After all, life brings many steps to take and long-term planning to commit to. Please do not stress yourself about time. With continuous effort and planning, you will get there.

As you refine your passions, do not fall into toxic crowds that engage in Oppression Olympics and excuses. That traps you in a never-ending cycle and destroys personal growth. I see far too many people who have been tainted by that cycle and it eats them on the inside.

Before I close, be kind and accepting of different opinions. I say that because the truth about the autism community is that everyone is their own individual. The community has never been a one-size-fits-all for group thinking, despite people believing so. It is okay to stand out.

Now, go forward and live your life!
Andrew Arboe

BIOGRAPHY:

Andrew Arboe is the Director of Community Outreach of Planning Across the Spectrum. He reaches out to autism organizations to start collaborations on empowering the community. Collaborations include setting up speaking engagements, being involved in conferences, or connecting organizations to Planning Across the Spectrums' services. Other work includes managing the free-to-use national calendar and writing blog posts on various autism topics. Andrew's special interest is driving, and he wants others to navigate the driving journey with more supports than he had. He helped inspire the first autism program within The Next Street, a driving school in Connecticut. In 2021, Andrew created Driving with Autism to move his work towards the national level. Please stay tuned to Driving with Autism's Facebook page for future updates on his webinar series and projects.

Being autistic himself, Andrew knows outcomes are like the ups and downs of the autism community. He aims to provide proactive values towards his work in the community. Andrew prefers the brick-and-mortar approach to managing transportation issues and promoting self-empowerment. He believes having people learn about self-help can make a major difference in their lives, more than waiting for an invisible force to make things better.

Andrew graduated from Manchester Community College with an associate degree as a disability specialist and is attending Charter Oak State College to earn a bachelor's degree in psychology. He hopes to get certified in autism and other related fields.

Email: andrew.arboe@autismdriving.com

Social Media

Facebook Driving with Autism: autisticdriving

LinkedIn: https://www.linkedin.com/company/autismdriving

Hashtag

#ForgeYourPath

FROM LOSS AND TRAGEDY TO JOY AND AUTISM

Nicole Gottesmann is a stay-at-home mom and blogger on Instagram and has a Facebook page and YouTube channel called, For the Love of Gabe.

"Unconditional love is the cure."

Sometimes it takes rock bottom, a sage yoga instructor, and strangers on the internet to lead you to love. Through love, I have learned more about what it means to live hopefully and with acceptance, even after tragedy. This story of unconditional love begins with my first pregnancy.

I loved being pregnant. I was twenty-nine years old

and ready for this new stage in my life. It felt like my whole life was meant for the baby I was growing inside of me. I'll never forget the reaction from my husband, Seth when I told him the good news. Later, when we found out we were having a boy I had never seen him so happy about anything! He was meant to be a dad! As we drove to Montauk for our third wedding anniversary, we decided on his name: Gavin Anthony Gottesmann.

When we got back from our vacation, I started bleeding. We learned too late that I had an incompetent cervix, and Gavin was born at twenty-three weeks. Seth and I had to bury our son three days after his birth.

I wanted a do-over.

I desperately needed to get pregnant again, hoping to ease the pain of this unthinkable tragedy. I believed that would be the only way I would survive losing our son. Seth wanted more time to heal but reluctantly agreed to try again. I got pregnant with Gabe quickly and at ten weeks gestation, I had a transabdominal cerclage placed to fix my cervix. Determined to carry this baby to full term and monomaniacally concerned with my own grief and anxiety, I missed the signs that something was wrong with Seth. The week before Christmas, we argued about Christmas trees. My family was coming up for the holiday and I wanted everything to be perfect including my Christmas tree. After having Seth go and buy a Christmas tree and set it up, I realized I would prefer a tree with white lights instead of colored lights. So, I sent Seth to take it down and return it for the tree I really wanted. He was rightfully frustrated and yelled, "I feel like I'm going to have a heart attack and never know my child!" I thought he was being overly dramatic while I was the one who was hormonal and stressed out.

On December 23, we had an appointment to find out our baby's gender. I had been gone about an hour before arriving home from a previous appointment when I noticed Seth face down in the balcony. He looked asleep, but I realized it was something more. When I went to him my worst suspicions were confirmed. Officially, Seth had a sudden cardiac arrhythmia, but I believe he died of a broken heart. While I tried to resuscitate him, all I could think of was that I was going to lose our baby, too. The trauma of finding Seth dead could cause me to miscarry. To be honest, I wondered if that would be for the best. How could I possibly survive losing a baby and my husband within five months of each other and maintain another pregnancy?

B-DAY

Gabe was born full-term with the help of the cerclage that kept my cervix intact. It was a huge relief! I had survived the hardest thing that I had ever faced. Gabe was the baby of my dreams! He was perfect and looked so much like his dad with blonde hair and blue eyes. That was when I stopped being afraid of being a single mom. How lucky was I to have a real live piece of Seth with me? I experienced joy and love at a level I was unaware existed prior to experiencing so much loss, and I also gained a greater appreciation for everything and everyone. I took nothing for granted, especially the opportunity to be a mother to Gabe. Gabe was going to be my little best friend and there were so many adventures I had planned for us. The beach and the mountains were calling!

D-DAY

Life changed direction again when Gabe turned a year old. I started to notice that he was developing at a slower pace than the other babies we saw at the mommy-and-me groups. Those babies were pointing; Gabe never pointed. When moms called their names, they all looked. Gabe never looked. These babies stopped babbling and started saying words. Gabe continued to struggle to get the words out. It was brought to my attention that these were all signs of autism, so I took Gabe to be evaluated. When Gabe was a little over a year old, the developmental pediatrician felt Gabe was too connected to me and took that as a sign he didn't have autism, but he wasn't sure and wanted to reevaluate. We came back at eighteen months, and it was determined that Gabe had autism. A few months later, I took Gabe to another evaluation at Kennedy Krieger Institute in Baltimore, Maryland. After six hours of evaluation, it was confirmed that Gabe had autism and was on the severe end of the spectrum! My heart sank. If I thought I was scared when I found my husband dead on the balcony at twelve-weeks pregnant, this was a much more terrifying situation. So many questions crossed my mind. How was I going to raise a severely autistic child all by myself? Would Gabe ever talk? Would I ever meet someone who would love us? What kind of a future would Gabe have? Would he have friends, get married, or have children of his own? Am I destined to live a life of loneliness? I also wondered if it was my fault that he had autism. After all, I had experienced a major traumatic event while he was in utero.

All the mom friends I thought I had made over that first year of motherhood were nowhere to be found. We had nothing in common anymore. Now, my life consists of driving Gabe from occupational therapy to speech therapy to Applied Behavior Analysis (ABA) therapy and a special school five days a week. My head was spinning, but I was again determined to fix something. I was going to get Gabe's diagnosis reversed by enrolling him in all the therapies recommended. I didn't have the strength to find out anything that might make me feel worse about the future. I refused to read about autism, talk about autism, or seek out any other people living like us. I had no friends who were parents of a child with autism. My plan was to do all the early intervention needed for Gabe to be cured so our life would get back to the way it was supposed to be! I envisioned Gabe in a regular school, able to talk, birthday party invitations overflowing our mailbox. I wanted so badly to blend in with the other moms and have a "normal" life again. I would make my comeback from being the pregnant widow in the neighborhood. I definitely did not want to be further known as the widowed mom with an autistic child.

My comeback involved a lot of self-care. I started practicing yoga. In yoga classes, I was able to shut my mind off from thinking about Gabe not talking. After a class one night, I was filling my instructor in on Gabe's progress in speech therapy; really, that there had been none. My instructor said something that has stayed with me for the last ten years: "I was thinking about what you are going through with Gabe. I think the solution is to love him unconditionally. That's the cure." Still absorbed in having Gabe's diagnosis reversed, I didn't understand how loving him unconditionally could be the cure. Accepting what is beyond my control and letting go has never been easy for me. However, I tried to take his advice.

ROCK BOTTOM

There is so much more to autism than being able to speak or not. For Gabe, one part of having autism is that he can't fall asleep and stay asleep easily, which meant I couldn't sleep either. I had no one to switch off with me or give me any break. Each night he would run around our apartment until the sun came up, causing chaos and destruction. I was so exhausted that I hit rock bottom. I turned to alcohol and anti-anxiety medication and found myself getting not one, but two DUIs. I knew what I needed to do. Gabe was three years old when I left him with family for thirty days and willingly went to rehab many states away.

ACCEPTANCE

Getting sober was the best thing that I ever did for myself and for Gabe. Accepting what I couldn't change became easier as I delved deeper into sobriety. I learned to be comfortable in my own skin for the first time. I cared much less about what other people thought about me or my circumstances. I started to accept not only Gabe but myself. I learned how to be open and honest about what I was going through as a single parent to an autistic child. I started to find people in the community who could relate to us, and life became a lot less lonely.

I also became more aware of the local autism community, and Gabe began to participate in activities for kids with autism. At five years old, he attended an inclusion camp where he had a one-on-one counselor, Sara. Attending summer camp was a dream come true for Gabe! It was like a switch had been flipped after that experience and a new side of Gabe appeared! His teenage counselor knew innately how to enter his world by showing him so much love and acceptance. This is when I started to understand what my yoga teacher was talking about! When Gabe was with Sara, he was his best self: happy, joyous, and singing! He started to hum songs here and there and used his voice frequently to talk in his own way. It's as though his life started when he met Sara at the Jewish Community Center Camp (JCC).

Gabe loved being with Sara, so I hired her after the summer as Gabe's babysitter. So much that was inside of him was beginning to come out. Sara taught me how to get Gabe to communicate with basic sign language and helped me create picture cards to help Gabe make requests. Gabe started to use an iPad with a communication app, which was truly life-changing. Gabe's behavior significantly changed once he had a way to communicate his needs clearly. School improved for Gabe, too once he received his communication device! Life was good again! Gabe was calm and content, not screaming and throwing himself into the furniture to get a point across because he could now tell me his wants and needs. I wish I had not been so afraid in the beginning to find out about autism, the therapies, ways nonverbal kids can learn to communicate, and how to meet my son's sensory needs. Once we figured that out, Gabe was happy and much more regulated!

Sara did not leave us hanging when she went to

college. She gave us the names of people, like her, who would love Gabe just as much. Personally, I think the most valuable thing in life is to have love in it, and Gabe has developed incredibly close and loving relationships with those who work with him after school. Finding the right help and network of people to care for Gabe has changed the trajectory of his life. A professional told me that Gabe would never have a close relationship with anyone other than me, but for years, Gabe has been surrounded by people who love and accept him, which has created a safe space for him to be himself. Gabe has so many people he loves, and he can hold on to that even when they are gone.

As I entered my third year of sobriety, I became more comfortable within myself, braver than before. I was ready to find someone to share our life. I had dated many men since Seth had passed away, and it occurred to me that maybe that wasn't the right path anymore. So, I changed the gender of who I was interested in on my Tinder dating profile from men to women. A first-grade teacher named Caroline came into our lives when Gabe was six. I was always afraid that anyone I was interested in would run for the hills if they knew I was not just a widow, but the sole parent of a severely autistic child. When I told Caroline all about Gabe on our second date, she was cool and unfazed. When they met, it was easy and natural. Gabe has always been easy to love for those willing to get to know him. I allowed myself to fall in love with her as I realized this could be real. Eventually, Gabe gained another mom! I never thought Gabe and I would ever find someone like Caroline, and she says she's the lucky one.

BUILDING A COMMUNITY

Feeling loved and accepted in this world is invaluable. One of the greatest gifts I've found along the way is the autism community through Instagram and Facebook. A community formed unexpectedly after I shared a video of Gabe and his babysitter on social media a few years ago. After receiving hundreds of messages from other parents, I realized that I was in the right place. I finally found my people! They were there the entire time. I just didn't know they existed! Instagram in particular is where I have found the most resources and information about autism. I have learned so much from followers and the pages I follow in this community. The community I cherish so much consists of autistic individuals, parents with autistic kids, educators, therapists, and others who care for someone with autism. I can honestly say I would know much less about my son if not for strangers on Instagram.

TODAY

Gabe is twelve years old and has started middle school. He is still severely impacted by autism, which means he needs help every step of the way. Yet, he has a presence that is truly special. When he stares into your eyes, he sees into your soul. He connects with people so easily if they are open to it. It's his gift. He may not talk, but he sings. As a nonspeaking person, Gabe communicates his feelings effortlessly. He is affectionate, which is one of my favorite things about him. Gabe is alive when music is playing, especially music by Queen and Kid Cudi. He is entirely and unapologetically himself. Always thinking, he has so much inside getting ready to come out. Currently, Gabe uses a communication device called Touch Chat. Soon he will learn how to spell through a teaching method called Rapid Prompting Method (RPM), which helps kids communicate by spelling on a letterboard. Whether it's through his own voice, a communication device, spelling, or typing, what matters most to me now is that he communicates to the best of his ability. I can't wait to hear what he has to say when he's ready!

Once I stopped trying to change Gabe and just love him, everything else changed! It's true what my yoga teacher said to me a decade ago. Unconditional love is the cure, and I have never felt more at peace. May you also find this unconditional love in your life and live it out for others.

Resources
- Ascendigo: www.ascendigo.org
- Camp JCC: www.benderjccgw.org/camp-jcc

Social Media

Facebook: For the Love of Gabe

Instagram: nicolegottesmann

YouTube: For the Love of Gabe

Hashtag

#ForTheLoveOfGabe

A Love Letter to Gabe

Dear Gabe,

I dreamt of you before you were born. Before you even existed! I imagined you at seven years old on a bus sitting with your dad. You were blonde, unable to speak, and struggling to stay in your seat. Your dad was having a hard time holding you. I woke up from that dream feeling afraid. Afraid for the wrong reasons. You see, I didn't know what it meant to have a child with autism at the time and I was convinced you were like this boy in my dream.

Back then, few knew what autism was, except as something to be afraid of. People are afraid of the unknown, and that is why I find it important (and love!) to share our experiences with strangers on the internet. I want the world to know you and all of the other kids like you. I want them to know that you belong. You are worthy of love, friendship, and a fulfilling future. We have a lot of work to do to change the perception of people with autism and to get you the accommodations you deserve, but I can already see the perception shifting.

If my dream had shown me more than a snapshot and included the true essence of who you are, I would not have been afraid to have an autistic son. I would have felt so grateful and excited to be your mother! You are loving, affectionate, smart, and intuitive. It doesn't come easy for you to use your voice, but when you do, it is the most beautiful sound I've ever heard. You've taught me so much, especially that communication comes in many forms. You can communicate so much with one look.

Gabe, I can't wait to see what your future holds. I sense that you are going to continue to make a meaningful difference in this world.

Love,
Mom

Photo Credit: Skye Prentice

BIOGRAPHY

Nicole Gottesmann is a stay-at-home mom and blogger on Instagram and has a Facebook page and YouTube channel, For the Love of Gabe. On YouTube, Nicole and her family share their lives as a family impacted by autism. Her inspiring posts and videos have an uplifting message: in spite of many obstacles, it is possible to have an amazing life full of love and hope.

A graduate of the University of Delaware with a degree in Hotel and Restaurant Management, Nicole married her college sweetheart, Seth, with whom she had two sons, Gavin and Gabriel.

After losing her first born prematurely, Nicole became pregnant again. Five months later, Nicole became a widow while pregnant with Gabriel. Gabriel was diagnosed with severe autism before two years old.

Nicole has been with her partner, Caroline Kiernan (who is also Gabe's mom!), for six years. They live in Gaithersburg, Maryland, with Gabe's best friend, their golden retriever, Bailey.

AM I MOM ENOUGH? CONTENDING WITH THE VOICES IN MY HEAD

Morénike Giwa Onaiwu is an advocate, public speaker, writer, educator, researcher, mom, and founder and principal operator of Advocacy Without Borders, a grassroots community nonprofit that encourages all people to make a difference.

"I believe in acceptance . . . but . . . the truth is that LIVING that acceptance in all areas of your life in all ways at all times—it's hard, and I don't always succeed."

Even though I (should) know better, sometimes it's hard not to feel like a failure.

Kids get older. Things change.

People change, and circumstances change.

Parenting is never easy—especially when you factor in disabilities, and my kids and I have many of those: autism, ADHD, psychological and neurocognitive conditions. But it gets even more complicated as the children grow. It's so different; a big change.

My kids are struggling. They're autistic. They don't like change. They're scared of change. They can't control change.

I'm struggling. I'm autistic. I don't like change. I'm scared of change. I can't control change . . .

So much of friendship for youth depends upon various factors, including communication and socialization, to be in place. And parents bear a lot of responsibility for ensuring that their child has certain skills to make friendship even possible.

Navigating the confusing social realm can be challenging for kids on the spectrum. This might require that we, as parents, really "step up" to help. Our kids might need us to help "bridge" the gap for them in several ways. We might have to put forth more effort . . . to arrange, facilitate, and develop connections.

It's especially important when it is apparent that your child can't—or won't—do it for themselves. Because that can provide a model for our kids, as well. But in my case, what complicates the matter further is that I'm not any good with any of these things. It's not that I am unwilling. It's because I can't do it.

I know I *need* to do it . . . because my kids can't do it for themselves. However, I can't do it either.

I'm not made that way . . . I'm not like other moms.

I can't be the room parent.

I can't chat it up every day at pick up and drop off with other parents.

I can't handle loud, crowded birthday parties.

I'm not savvy enough to score playdates with classmates for my kids.

I haven't heard that song or read that magazine article.

I haven't watched that show or that sports game.

I don't have cooking or decorating tips I can share.

I am anxious about lock-ins, sleepovers, and other activities where I can't assure my kids' safety.

I don't like being out in the elements. Too much sun creates headaches. Too much cold hurts. Too many smells and sounds are overwhelming. Wind, insects, sleeping outside on flimsy fabric on rocky ground . . . not my idea of fun.

I don't share most people's fascination with celebrities, certain genres of music, movies, or video games.

I'm not skilled at vacuous conversation just for the sake of filling up space or passing time.

I don't want to wear something uncomfortable just to appear trendy.

I don't like having to scrutinize every other word I say.

I get drained regulating my vocal tone to a pitch and prosody others find "normal" while policing myself to avoid topics I enjoy because others find them "weird."

I hate trying to determine how many seconds of pausing is appropriate.

I worry whether the forced eye contact I'm making passes for natural or looks creepy.

I don't like not having a plan.

I don't like the sensation of my pulse racing and my temperature rising as I fight to conjure the ability, maybe successfully this time, not to give off vibes that reveal how very different, how anxious, how frightened I am when engaging in pastimes I dislike, but most find enjoyable.

Most of all, I hate that it's like this . . . that *I'm* like this, because it would be easier for you, my beloved babies, if I could be more like *them*. It would give you a fighting chance, instead of neither you all nor I knowing what the hell we're doing.

Good Lord—why is this so damn hard?

You all are the loves of my life. The lights of my eyes. I adore you, even when you have stinky feet and a funky attitude. You're my perfectly imperfect not-so-little-anymore creations. My "mini-mes," yet each still wholly *you*. My awesomely autistic wonders.

I would walk through fire for you, without regret, if you needed me to. Without a moment of hesitation. I'd do anything for you.

I want so much for you.

I want you to be safe.

I want you to feel proud.

I want you to be happy.

I want you to have friends.

You need friends, right? All kids do, probably. Right?

Isn't that a core part of life, development, coming of age?

Sometimes you seem content alone or with family. But I also sense that maybe you want more?

Maybe it's more than a want; maybe it's more of a need?

One that is continuously unmet, and I'm not doing a good job at fulfilling it for you?

You look at me, and you see familiarity. You are at ease. Is this my fault?

By cultivating you to think it's okay to be you—for me to be me—have I messed you up?

Maybe one day you aren't going to *want* to be like you? Maybe it's not good for you to be like me? Maybe you want to be kind of like them too? They're normal. I'm never gonna be.

How do I get you, friends?

How do I do this? How?

How do I play the game right, so these moms won't think I'm a freak, so they will consider letting you in?

If we pass that barrier, I still don't know if you will make friends with any of those other kids.

Maybe you won't have anything in common.

Maybe it's too much hassle.

Maybe they will think you're weird—and then I will shut the whole thing down, because I'm not going to let anyone shun you or make you feel less than. And maybe that's part of the problem too, that I'd rather you be alone and safe than surrounded by friends who hurt you. But then again, is that my choice to make for you?

And is it the right choice?

Just thinking about this is so tiresome and so draining.

Maybe the idea is draining for you, too, and that might be why you don't have friends.

Yet, you're so funny, so wonderful, so unique. You'd make a great friend.

I hope I'm not signaling to you that you need to have a friend to validate who you are.

Then I wonder about timing and circumstances. It might not be that you aren't making efforts. Maybe you're nervous. Maybe you're worried about being rejected. Maybe you exert the emotional energy, the "spoons,"[2] to try something new. Like meeting with a classmate or doing an activity you aren't accustomed to or going into an unfamiliar environment—it might just feel like too much. Which I can understand.

And yet, maybe . . .

---

[2] Schultz, Kirsten. "I'm a 'Spoonie.' Here's What I Wish More People Knew About Chronic Illness," Healthline, April 18, 2019. https://www.healthline.com/health/spoon-theory-chronic-illness-explained-like-never-before#1

Maybe . . . maybe . . . maybe.

Argh!!! This is too much. It's too much.

Actually, it's not too much. It's me, stressing over this. I'm the thing that's too much.

I'm too much. Of everything.

Too much for everyone, maybe even myself. I overthink everything, overdo everything, over-stress over everything—and end up accomplishing nothing.

The mom stuff. The small talk.

I can do it in small doses.

But I can't sustain not being me over time. And I have to be me. I want to be me. Right?

But for you . . . I will do anything. I will do anything for you. Anything.

I would be something else, someone else, if I could. I will, if I can.

If it would help me fit in better, to benefit you.

Just to gain you access, get you through the door. I just want to get you past the barrier, get you entry. Get the world to look past what they perceive as oddity, and truly see you.

Because you are so, so amazing.

I believe that once you are inside—I pray—how wonderful you are will be apparent.

I just need to get them to see you—really see you.

I don't want to be a hypocrite. I don't want to be one of those "Do as I say, not as I do" people. All your life I have preached the importance of being your true self, the importance of acceptance; how there's nothing at all wrong with the way you are. But I don't know if my idealistic teachings are simply setting you up for a lifetime of disappointment. I don't know if principle over practicality will make your life harder. That's not what I want.

Hark! The words of a hypocrite, your mother. Don't conform, my loves. Don't change.

Don't compromise yourself. Don't be like me.

Just be you. I will be whatever the world needs me to be, however fake I need to be—for you, although I pray you're never aware of that. This is my choice. You're worth it.

But don't take this mantle upon yourself. Don't ever affix this mask to your face; you might not be able to remove it.

Don't change. Please, don't change. I only want you to be YOU. Don't change for anyone. You are perfect. Do as I say, not as I do—don't be like me.

So, here we are . . .

I am despondent, weary—nearing implosion. Internal devastation—camouflaged with a trained smile, an air of feigned confidence, and a thin yet convincing veneer of "success."

But I'm a fraud.

One who can address the United Nations, command the attention of world leaders—yet cannot effectively go through the motions to obtain a playdate for my babies.

It hurts.

I try. And fail. And then because I have previously failed, I am plagued with trepidation and doubt.

Which makes it even harder to try again.

Which makes me suck at it even more.

You don't have any friends. At least I don't think you do. You sit alone at lunch, at recess. No one ever calls or texts. No one ever comes over. You aren't invited to parties or outings. No one comments on or likes your posts. You perseverate over things; dive deep into your hobbies. You're overly self-critical. Is any of that due to not having friends?

I don't bring it up, so as to not make you uncomfortable, and you seldom mention it.

Often, you don't seem to care.

Is that normal?

Am I making you friendless, abnormal?

You smile every day. Is it real?

Are you really happy? Is this enough for you?

Am I giving you enough, showing you enough? Am I trying hard enough? Doing enough? For you?

My beloved children. Some of you hail from the waters of my womb; some of you were hand-woven into my heart; love and DNA are equal in strength.

My loves. You are the reason I draw breath.

Am I failing you?

How can I help you do something I don't even know how to do?

How can I teach you something I have never been good at?

How can I get them—other kids—to accept you, to want to know you, to like you, when I can't navigate the parent layer that guards the gate?

People socialize in different ways. Deep down inside me, I know there's nothing wrong with who I am, with how I am. That even if I wasn't an autistic mom, I shouldn't have to feel forced to conform to contrived social and gender norms of how a parent is "supposed to be" supporting one's children in having friendships.

I know this . . . cognitively.

But that doesn't make me immune to the messages whispering that I am nothing like what I am supposed to be as a mother.

That I'm doing it all wrong.

That I am making them social misfits.

So much fear—that my failure to do these things that seem to come so easily to other parents will, and already does, have a negative impact on all of you. That you are going to suffer in life because of this, because of me. What does that mean for you, for your future? What does that say about me? Am I an inadequate mother?

Am I "mom" enough?

I battle these voices in my head constantly. The messages. The fears. The guilt. That tells me I'm not mom enough; not good enough. Just not enough.

These voices are lies. But they sure as hell sing a convincing song—like the tune of sirens ushering sailors to their death. I must stay afloat. I must.

My kids have autism. That's never going to change. I have autism; that's never going to change. And why should we have to change in order to be accepted by the rest of the world? Why can't the rest of the world change too, meet us where we are, and accept us? All we want—all we need—is acceptance. Nothing more, nothing less. Why does it seem like it would be easier to find the pot of gold at the end of a rainbow than for us to be accepted like we are, as who we are, autism and all? We deserve acceptance. Acceptance.

Acceptance.

I believe in acceptance. I write about acceptance. I present about acceptance. I teach about acceptance.

But if I'm going to be real with myself, and with you, the truth is that LIVING that acceptance in all areas of your life in all ways at all times—it's hard, and I don't always succeed.

I don't have answers to any of the questions raised by the voices in my head. I still don't know if they're right—should I put on a façade to make the path of your lives smoother or be my real self despite the inherent risk in that? I still don't know if I'm doing any of this right or wrong.

I do know this: I want so much for you. But if I could

choose only one thing that I could guarantee for you, I know what I'd choose. What any parent would choose for their child, regardless of neurology. I'd choose for you to be happy.

Contending with the voices in my head sucks. They weigh so heavily on me. They guilt me, shame me, confuse me. I hope you never, ever develop such hateful, self-deprecating internal voices, and that you never, ever experience anything like this. I don't want you to ever go through what I went through—what I still go through. I don't want you to ever feel broken. I don't want you to ever BE broken.

I don't want you to ever know what it's like. Ever. To live with these voices in your head.

I didn't ask for them, true—their seeds were implanted, unbeknownst to me, by the world in my youth. But unfortunately, they have been incubated and nourished over the years by my own self-doubt. By my own fears. And like any parasitic organism, it depletes the energy of its unwilling host. It is a very toxic relationship indeed.

I hate those voices so much.

If they ever come whispering to you, ignore them. The voices lie, convincingly. They know just what to say, and just how to say it, to entrap you in fear. They are extraordinarily skilled at deception. In time, their lies no longer sound like lies. They begin to sound, and feel, like the truth.

The voices say that you're not enough, never enough. They make me wonder which of us is right . . . me or them. They make me wonder if just being me—as I am—is good for you. Is right for you. Is enough for you.

I don't know how to silence them. Maybe I never will. But I can, and will, learn how to pointedly ignore them. They are lies. The love I see in your eyes, in your smiles, in your gleeful flapping hands: that's the truth.

For you, I will fight to become what you need. I will be mom enough.

I just want to be the mom you need—without losing me. Somehow, I will find my way.

Resource
- https://morenikego.com/faq

Website: morenikego.com/contact

Hashtag
#Neurodiversity

My Love Letter to Autism

Dear Autism,

The world hates you, you know.
Fears and despises you;
Wants to prevent you.
They say that you are a tremendous source
Of "suffering." Despair. Devastation.
They detest you, just like they loathe
The melanin that warms my skin;
The curls and kinks that sprout defiantly from my scalp;
The curvy voluptuousness of my lips and hips;
The rhythmic flair of my movements and speech;
The slant of my eyes and high roundness of my cheeks.
All my life, these things about me
These things that are different
Have been labeled "bad"
And, therefore, worthy of hatred.
But hate is not what I feel.
Not for myself
And not for you.
I'm not fooled.
You see, I recognize their hatred.
I've known since the day of my birth
How much the world fears
And feels threatened
By that which is different.

That which they don't understand;

That which they cannot control.

They see difference, and instantly think, "Bad."

Their first instinct is to fix! Alter!

And if unsuccessful, eradicate.

Wipe it away; get rid of it. Purge it.

Six letters…

Autism.

Such a simple word, autism.

How . . . how could I ever hate you?

You are part of my mother;

Part of my grandfather;

Part of my children

And part of me.

Yeah, sometimes you get on my d@mn nerves…

But I don't

And I won't

And I will never

Hate you.

And no matter what the world says or thinks,

I know you embody and amplify love from within.

And together, we're gonna be all right.

BIOGRAPHY

Morénike Giwa Onaiwu, PhD, MA, is an educator, writer, public speaker, parent, and global advocate whose work focuses on meaningful community involvement and leadership, disability, racial, and gender equity, dismantling stigma, and inclusion and empowerment. Often drawing from personal background as a person of color in a neurodiverse and serodifferent family, a late-diagnosed adult on the autism spectrum, and relevant educational and professional experience, Morénike is a highly sought-after presenter, consultant, and subject matter expert.

Morénike, founder and principal operator of Advocacy Without Borders, has been an invited speaker in the White House, at the United Nations Headquarters, a keynote speaker and/or presenter at numerous conferences, and provides diversity, research, and disability consulting to several organizations. Morénike, a humanities scholar at Rice University, has been published by Beacon Press and Palgrave MacMillan and will release a 2023 edited collection on neurodiversity in the Black community with Jessica Kingsley Publishing.

Morénike and spouse reside in the U.S. Gulf Coast and proudly parent six beautiful biological and internationally adopted "tween" to young adult children, all of whom have hidden disabilities.

SHARING A JOYFUL LIFE

Valerie Brooks is the founder of Autistic Interpretations®, a social media community that spans a blog, Instagram, YouTube, and Facebook. In her daily posts, Valerie shares and celebrates a joyful life of everyday experiences with her autistic blind daughter and the strong, loving village that surrounds them.

"Progress never stops."

Life is not how I thought it would be. For a long time, I thought my daughter Jessica would eventually learn academics. At the very least, by the time she aged out of public school, I expected we would find a job for Jess that fit her skillset. I did not expect us to lose the academic battle, to fail to find a job placement, to be completely unsuccessful with independent living skills, and to run out of options for safe and appropriate daily care for Jess.

I never expected to give up my nursing career to become the full-time caregiver for my adult, autistic, blind daughter. After decades of this advocacy life, I never expected to still feel deep down in the core of my being that there is no one in the world who understands how hard it is all day, every day.

And while I always felt a deep love and joy in my connection to Jess, I never expected to find a life that included happiness. Most certainly, I did not expect to be sharing a whole joy-filled life. Thirty-four years in, this is my autism story.

WE DON'T ALL MOURN THE SAME WAY, NOR FOR THE SAME REASON

Other parents have told me that receiving their child's autism diagnosis was experienced as a devastating loss. I was not one of those parents. In fact, experiencing diagnosis as a loss never occurred to me until much later in life. My autistic daughter, Jessica, was already an adult when I read about other parents grieving. Frankly, even though I had seen my mother's grief on the day of Jessica's first diagnosis, I was bewildered about this grief and couldn't relate.

Until one day I could. In my case, grieving came after many years of fighting, following all of the failures.

WHY DID I GRIEVE SO MUCH LATER?

In Jessica's early years, we were busy fighting. Autism diagnoses were not common in the late 1980s, and it turns out they were particularly difficult to diagnose in blind toddlers and in girls. We had to fight for years to get the diagnosis. For us, Jessica's autism diagnosis at seven years old was a win, but only briefly. What followed was a series of fights to get the diagnosis recognized by the school system. The fight that we thought would be mostly behind us after the diagnosis never really ended.

To understand our story, you need to know that Jessica is medically complex. Not only is she autistic but she has a brain malformation, which is the root cause of her cortical blindness and developmental disability. These diagnoses are woven together, difficult to separate, yet the combination is exponentially more challenging compared to the sum of the separate parts. To further complicate Jessica's reality, she also has minor fine motor and gross motor deficits. The wonder of Jessica's medical complexity took years to unravel.

Jessica was a typical cute baby. We were young parents. My mom was the first person who noticed there was something different about Jessica. When she was six months old, we learned Jessica had cortical blindness. The exact and unforgettable words from the pediatrician were, "This baby is blind and forevermore will be."

Our first real introduction to advocacy was to convince the neurosurgeon to attempt an intervention relating to hydrocephalus. Our insistence paid off and the surgery was completed. We would learn later that it gave Jess a tiny, vague, and unknowable window into a sighted world. Despite that success, Jessica is blind, and it is difficult to overstate the impact her blindness has had on subsequent diagnoses and learning opportunities. Importantly, Jessica's blindness meant that it took more convincing that she was different beyond her vision impairment.

We kept fighting because it meant access to services—or so we thought at the time. We always believed in Jessica's potential and held out hope for the system of therapies and education. While fighting for Jess, I also persevered and completed my nursing degree. I always believed in a future where there was a place for Jessica to contribute to society and for me to achieve my own potential. I had spent years fighting, becoming an advocacy champion, leaving no time nor space for grieving.

My grieving began as Jessica aged out of the school system. Long-anticipated milestones of independence and contribution did not come, and it all felt like failure.

RUNNING OUT OF OPTIONS

Jessica was in public school from the time she was four years old through her twenty-first year. Individualized Education Programs (IEPs) were a way of life, and I attended at least forty. Our family had a strong support system that led to good information about advocacy and our parental rights. We knew how to go into an IEP empowered and prepared. You would think we would have had enough experience with failure through the school years to take nothing for granted, but there had always been the hope of and belief of good options for Jessica.

As planned, when Jess aged out of school, I finally had my nursing degree and had started working as a registered nurse. All along, I had allowed myself to envision a fulfilling future for Jess and me. I had imagined what it could be like to have some flexibility and some freedom from this eternal responsibility that I had readily embraced for so long.

But we quickly ran out of options for Jessica, including options for daily care. We tried, but the reality is that Jessica did not have the required skills for independence or contribution in a job setting. I know this because in addition to the work of therapists and teachers, I have worked with her for more than three decades, trying to teach her skills for independence and vocation. For adults like Jessica with a lack of self-care, self-help, and independent living skills, there are safety factors, such as risk of fire from trying to cook, risk of physical and sexual abuse, risk of wandering (magnified by cortical blindness), and the list goes on and on.

The reality I had been holding onto for thirty years came crashing back down, and I felt such defeat—such massive discouragement. I wanted to give up, to withdraw, and to isolate myself. So, that's what happened, and I allowed it. It is what I needed—for a while.

I NEED TO LIVE FOREVER

Like most special-needs parents, I feel the urgent need to live a long time. Yet the reason I need to live a long time is the reason I probably will not. Autism life has meant chronic, every-single-day stress. Chronic stress has serious consequences. It can cause or exacerbate inflammation, fatigue, and illness. As a single parent of a dependent adult with disabilities, stress has been a major factor for most of my life.

I also have struggled my entire life with depression, but things became even more complicated when I was diagnosed with an autoimmune condition. Soon after that diagnosis, I developed pneumonia for the first time and the recovery process was much longer and more difficult than I ever would have expected. Something had to give.

Finally, I mourned the loss of expectations. And after all those years, I joined the list of parents who grieved their child's diagnosis. After all those years of fighting, I hit a wall. It felt like complete failure: failure to find a day program for Jessica, failure to find meaningful contribution for Jessica, and failure to apply my nursing credentials as a career. My health gave up and so did I.

CAN THERE BE SUCCESS FROM THE SUM OF FAILURES?

After some tough years and processing time, I was able to reflect and realize that what I had actually been grieving was *perceived* failure. Because while there were certainly failures along the way, we did not have to *end* with the failures. We had the option to keep trying to find what worked, to find the successes.

After that cycle of hopes, dreams, reality, and disappointment, I knew I had to figure something out. There must be some solution where Jessica feels like she is more independent, and I have more time to live life, I reasoned. I reached out to Jessica's Support Coordinator for help. When he visited, I did not hold back one bit. I explained my whole thought cycle, including my concerns about my physical and mental health.

"What are our options? I need help," I flatly but emphatically repeated. "I cannot do all of this anymore; it is killing me," I ended my plea.

JUST LIKE THAT, HOPE

Jessica's support coordinator was wonderful; a

genuine, kind, and caring person. He listened to me and heard me. I had said that I needed help and a weight was lifted. The meeting was encouraging, and I felt that he understood the depth of my strain. This was the beginning of creating a personalized care plan for Jessica. Once again, there was hope.

Thankfully, I acquired a small contract and was able to work from home. Soon after, I also started a blog, Autistic Interpretations, as a way to process what I was going through. The contracting job and the blogging turned out to be complementary and reinforcing so that I was able to grow my skill set.

It's not how I had imagined my life. But, through perseverance, adaptation, and help from others, we slowly found success. And I found peace.

THE PEACE OF ACCEPTANCE

When did I find acceptance? This is an important part of my autism story. I still remember the day. It was sometime after we had run out of options. As with most other days throughout her whole life, I was working on teaching Jess steps towards independence in the shower. At the time, I had been working on this goal for most of her twenty-eight years, and we had made little progress.

On that day, I let myself accept that independence in the shower wasn't going to happen for Jess. Part of acceptance was also personal, as in self-preservation.

It was a different feeling than defeat or lack of attaining a goal. Out of nowhere, I experienced the peace of acceptance.

PARADOXICALLY, THE SUM OF OUR FAILURES EQUALED SUCCESS

Without the road we had traveled, we wouldn't have ended in what now is our perfect place. That perfect place is me working from home, managing and supervising Jessica's daily care, and finding the peace of acceptance.

Getting to our perfect place included important resources, like family and our #GoodOnesFam. The most important and amazing thing we have done is to build a wonderful community of support through Autistic Interpretations. What started as a simple blog, an outlet, connected us with those who Jessica has affectionately dubbed #GoodOnes—amazing moms, dads, aunts, uncles, grandparents, teachers, aides, counselors, and professionals who let us know they understand, or identify, or have questions and want to know more. *Because of them, I have never again felt alone in this journey.*

But what about Jess? Is our current situation a failure or win for her? Jessica is now in a stable daily environment perfectly tailored to her needs. An environment with love and understanding that gives her flexibility and the support she needs to thrive. I can say with 100 percent certainty that for Jess, we are in a win-win-win, because:

1. **Her frustration and anxiety are at an all-time low.** We can avoid triggers and adjust as needed. When frustration and anxiety are low, life is better, and growth can occur.
2. **She has opportunities to engage.** She connects with a community, which has helped build her communication skills.
3. **Jess has purpose.** We have successfully tapped into Jessica's caregiving instincts since our virtual community has turned into the perfect platform for Jess to contribute in a way that resonates with her.

PROGRESS NEVER STOPS

At age thirty-four, Jessica is thriving. So am I. I have learned that progress never stops. Success may look different than we dreamed of for so many years, but progress was possible when I let go of my preconceived ideas and learned to ask for help.

I learned that purpose is powerful. My purpose is more than to look after Jessica, and importantly, Jessica has found a way to apply her caregiving instincts by connecting to a diverse and compassionate community. We live a life rich with accommodations, friendship, family, laughter, and the ordinary. Jessica and I both continue to grow, and while neither of us knows what the future holds, I can see the power of community and pursuing one's gifts with courage.

My Love Letter to Jessica

Jess,

My heart was opened up wide as soon as I knew you existed. For your whole life, I've been completely open, vulnerable, and expressive with the depth of my love for you. I believe, because of that, you know deep within your being just how much I love you.

What you may not understand is how you saved me. Within me, you filled the emptiness that I had always felt, the lack of belonging or place in this crazy world we live in. Suddenly, I had purpose. I was your mom. It was my place, and I was fiercely present for you.

You, my precious child and partner in life, have filled me with joy every single day, from your curls, smile, and dimples; your giggles, squeals, and happy noises; your pure, compassionate, and unconditionally loving being. What I want for you, now as well as long after I am gone, is to always feel respected, understood, cared for, and unconditionally and deeply loved in return.

It's important for you to know that life's stresses and hard moments have never been because of you. It has always been for you. And, you have been worth every single moment.

With love,
Mama

BIOGRAPHY

Based in the Chattanooga, Tennessee, area, Valerie Brooks, BSN, R.N., is the founder of Autistic Interpretations®, a social media community spanning a blog, Instagram, YouTube, and Facebook. A mother of three adult children, Valerie is the primary caregiver to her fully dependent, autistic, and legally blind adult daughter, Jessica. Together, they share a glimpse into their lives, rich with family, poodles, and southern cooking. Their posts reflect the joys and struggles of life with an adult autistic family member.

Having achieved her hard-won registered nurse designation and working in cardiac care, Valerie made the courageous decision to leave nursing to work from home and ensure Jessica would thrive. Through a steadfast commitment to sharing varied, authentic posts, Valerie has built an online community of more than 100 thousand subscribers. The goal of the #GoodOnes community is to share Val and Jessica's version of "normal" to show that it is good, and that progress never stops.

Beyond frequent challenges and frustrations, they find joy, entertainment, lessons, laughs, and good times. Valerie and Jess both actively engage with their #GoodOnes followers, and it has enriched their lives beyond their wildest expectations.

Contact
Autistic Interpretations, P.O. Box 28025,
Chattanooga, Tennessee 37424

Website: autisticInterpretations.com
Email: val@autisticinterpretations.com

Social Media
Facebook: autisticinterpretations
Instagram: autistic_interpretations
YouTube: Autistic Interpretations

Hashtags
#GoodOnesFam #GoodOnes #AutisticInterpretations

OUR SIBLING PERSPECTIVES

Hannah Brooks is an ASL/English interpreter and co-creator on Autistic Interpretations, a social media community that spans a blog, Instagram, YouTube, and Facebook.

"This is the life that I chose. This is the life that I worked so hard to make a reality."

A SISTER'S PERSPECTIVE

For most of my life, when anyone asked me what it was like to grow up with a sister with autism, I never knew what to say. It was just my life; it was the only thing I'd ever known. Everything I experienced was just my normal. I never had anything to compare it to, so how was I supposed to explain what it was like?

I always considered my childhood to be average. Not average in a not-awesome way, just not significantly different or abnormal compared to those of my friends and peers. My sister, Jessica, was always included in family activities and outings, we had family dinners all together, we played together, and we were together for all the things I considered to be "normal" family activities. As far as I remember, my parents never sat us down and said, "Our family is different and here's why."

Throughout my childhood, both Jessica and my brother always seemed to get more attention than I did, both from my parents and others around us. This never bothered me in the slightest, and in fact, I was often relieved to be more in the background, not the center of attention. Jessica's autism and other disabilities meant that she always *needed* more attention than I did. I didn't feel ignored, neglected, or left-out because of Jessica's needs. I was always confident in the knowledge that they were *needs*. I knew my parents loved me and would do anything for me, just as they would for Jessica and my brother.

It's easy for an outsider to say that having a sibling with autism would have a significant impact on my development, and of course it did. The positive impacts greatly dominated. There are too many to name, but the biggest one is the perspective on life that loving her brings. The happiness that Jessica brings to me is immeasurable. She carries a sense of unbridled joy, and it's truly wonderful to witness.

What negatively impacted me was witnessing the relationship and interactions between Jessica and our dad and Jessica and our brother; both relationships (although much improved now that we are all adults) have always been complicated. Any leftover feelings of bitterness, resentment, and unfairness I have are more connected to my brother, with whom I always have had a complicated relationship. As a child, I couldn't comprehend why my brother and father didn't understand Jessica in the way that my mom and I did, why my brother couldn't understand that Jessica needed the extra attention in a way that we didn't. I know now that my brother's childhood feelings and perspective were just as valid as mine were, and that his feelings weren't wrong just because they were different from mine.

While as a child I never truly understood how different my life was from my peers, now that I am an adult, those differences are much more apparent. In my career, I made friends my age both with and without children. I'm unsure how to put into words the stark difference I noticed between my life and theirs. My friends without children, who are financially responsible, hardworking career-women, seemed to have no responsibilities beyond working and paying the bills. They were free to go places and to do things whenever they wanted, to spend time together with our friends and to go shopping and to dinner. Even my friends with children could simply get a babysitter and do all these same things or bring their child along.

When I noticed these things, for the first time in my life it felt unfair. By my own choice, I had recently moved back home to live with Jessica and our mom. I didn't have the same freeness of schedule that my friends had. I needed to be home, to help with Jessica, to help my mom with the house, and choosing to go out with my friends instead often left me with a sense of guilt. For the first time, I realized that I have enormous responsibilities in my life that none of my friends have. While I felt guilty for spending time with friends because I was worried that I was shirking my responsibilities at home, I also felt worried and insecure every time I said no to my friends because I needed to be home. I was worried they would stop inviting me, stop being friends with me, because I so often had to say no. (Thankfully, I have wonderful, kind, and understanding friends.)

These feelings, changing my career, and the general stress that comes with being a caregiver to a person with autism left me with strong anxiety, stress, guilt, unfairness, and many other feelings that I struggle to name. These same friends became the resource and trigger for a turning point. One morning, I woke with a realization that changed all of this for me:

This is the life that I chose. This is the life that I worked so hard to make a reality.

While I didn't choose to be born a sister to a person with autism, I did choose everything else. I chose to live here and help take care of my sister. I chose to accept the lifelong responsibility that comes with it. I chose to make my family and my sister my top priority. I chose to let go of these negative feelings and instead focus on the positives. Jessica brings an immense joy and purpose to my life that others don't know or understand, but I do. And that makes me immeasurably lucky.

I love her. I love my family. This is what I want. This is a life that I love.

A BROTHER'S PERSPECTIVE

I asked my brother about his perspective, and this is what he said:

"When I look back furthest in my memory, I experience memories of growing up in a small but comfortable home with my sisters and parents. I was born several years after Jessica and roughly a year and a half before my younger sister, so I don't have any clear memories of my life without two sisters.

"I have plentiful positive memories of my childhood, and overall, I think it was a good one, but there were many frustrations and challenges for me. Nearly always, it felt like Jessica's needs were so many and often so LOUD that she was prioritized. Of course, as an adult looking back, I understand why this was on an intellectual level.

"Jessica is physically and intellectually disabled and incapable of many of the things I could do, even as a child. These capacities allowed me to make sense of the world and interact with it to creatively solve problems and to overcome issues that would send Jessica into a meltdown. This is why she required more attention and care, and why so often family plans did revolve (and still do) around Jessica's needs and desires.

"It seems to me strange to expect a young child to understand this. It felt unfair to me because, as a child, I didn't appreciate how different Jessica was from me. I believe I have always primarily viewed her as my sister, not as a disabled individual my family and I care for. And because of this, my child's mind did feel that it was unfair for Jessica to dominate the family dynamic, and I am sure this had a significant impact on my own development into adulthood. Additionally, as anyone familiar with developmental psychology knows, patterns laid in childhood don't disappear merely because a person matures into possessing adult-level reasoning abilities.

"However, as I have aged, I have come to balance these leftover feelings of unfairness with a wider perspective. Jessica did not do anything to lead to her disabilities, just as I did nothing to be born with an intact and healthy brain. Since I am not superstitious, I do not believe there is a deeper reason preceding these facts; bad and good things happen, and then we get to interpret them after the fact to build our life perspective. I, and I suspect most people, would rather have their full mental capacities intact to be able to live independent lives and overcome obstacles in life more fully, to appreciate complex novels and classical music instead of spending countless hours of their adult lives listening to Barney songs on repeat. But Jessica is also frequently deliriously happy and can feel extreme, real joy in people, both things I do not experience. If you take a view of life that happiness and suffering can balance, is she, on average, happier than many people with intact, healthy brains?

"The above is an example of the reflection that my experiences with Jessica have led to, which I believe have been invaluable. Anyone can follow a train of reasoning such as I laid out above, but the real teacher for me has been the interplay of my memories, my emotional response, and my reason.

"Even in adulthood, family life with Jessica in the mix has not been easy. Watching her mature due to a mix of strategies that have developed in the family over time, largely under the guidance of our mother, has been rewarding; that helps significantly. Still, things can be frustrating and challenging. But I realize that many without Jessica's challenges can offer significant trials for their families for other reasons, such as a substance abuse disorder or involvement in crime. And those trials don't have the silver lining that Jessica's do—Jessica's quirks and foibles aren't of her own making and can be frequently amusing and heartwarming.

"Jessica remains the central feature of the life of my family. There is a blog about her, multiple online platforms, and countless videos watched by thousands for amusement and education. She is the oldest chronologically, but, due to her dependence on others for help, remains the baby of the family. Every year I am more and more OK with this. I am far from perfect, and thus frequently unsuccessful at reminding myself that Jessica cannot help how she is, but I can change how I am. Perhaps this is the most important thing I can learn."

THE GOOD ONES FAM

Two siblings from the same family, with the same upbringing, can have such different perspectives. I have always been vastly different from my brother. We are individuals who need and feel differently, and both our perspectives and feelings are valid. While our views are certainly different, neither of us is right or wrong. I imagine it was hard for my mother to give the three of us what we needed when our needs were always so different.

I think that's a big reason why my mom started blogging about our family's autism story—as a form of therapy. The vast outpouring of love, support, and appreciation she received was wholly unexpected. Through the years, our community has gained a following we lovingly refer to as The Good Ones Fam. These are people of all ages, some with loved ones with special needs and some without. They are our cheerleaders on the good days and the hard days, and many of them have become our friends. They bring their perspectives just as my brother and I bring ours. The Good Ones Fam has opened our eyes to just how kind the world can be.

Over time, we began sharing our story with a new purpose: to show other autism families that life with a dependent autistic adult can be a joyful one. Yes, some days are hard. But we get through those hard days because Jessica fills our lives with an immense and unbridled joy that we now get to share with the world. We are happy.

Resources

- Autistic Interpretations: autisticinterpretations.com
- My best resource in my journey has been my mom—in this blog she has documented our autism story since Jess was born. The site is especially helpful for parents of newly diagnosed children as they learn how to advocate for those with special needs.

My Love Letter to My Sister

Dear Jessica,

I struggle to find the words that will encompass what you mean to me. You've brought such an immeasurable amount of joy into my life. I love watching you find joy, happiness, and light in the simplest of things. It really puts into perspective what matters in life. You have a way of seeing the best in people that I lack, and that's something I greatly admire. You taught me so many things, the greatest of which is an immense love that I don't feel with anyone else. Through you I learned responsibility at a young age, and that has shaped my life in a hugely positive way.

My wish for you is that someday your anxiety will be greatly diminished and you can feel more of a sense of peace. I hope that you are always able to feel the joy. I hope that you always feel safe and loved.

What I want you to know is this: I will always love you. I will always protect you. I will always support you. I will always be there for you. No matter what happens, you will always have me. For the rest of my life, I will do my absolute best to ensure you feel happy, loved, and safe. You are the light of my life.

Hannah

BIOGRAPHY

Based in the Chattanooga, Tennessee, area, Hannah is the youngest of three children. She is a certified ASL/English interpreter and a co-creator on Autistic Interpretations, a social media community that spans a blog, Instagram, YouTube, and Facebook. She graduated magna cum laude from Valdosta State University with a bachelor of science in education in American Sign Language/English Interpreting.

Hannah has been a full-time nanny and is a life-long caregiver to her sister with autism. She enjoys quiet days at home with her family, as well as family trips to the mountains, Disney World, and the beach. One of Hannah's greatest joys is her ten-month-old poodle puppy, Daryl.

Contact
Autistic Interpretations, P.O. Box 28025, Chattanooga, Tennessee 37424

Website: autisticinterpretations.com

Social Media
Instagram: hannahbroooks

Hashtags
#DarylThePoodlePup #GoodOnes #GoodSister

THE HEALING POWER OF AUTISM

Kacie Wielgus Buzzard is the founder of therapymom.co, a community for parents raising autistic kids and a contributor to The Mighty and Kveller. Kacie serves as a pro-bono education advocate and leads social media for an international company. Connect with her on LinkedIn, Twitter, or therapymom.co to talk about your parenting experiences with autism.

"Autism taught us to control what we must, plan for what we can, and learn to embrace the unexpected."

An immigrant growing up on the South Side of Chicago with an abusive stepfather and an alcoholic mother, my dad was quick to temper by the time I was born. I used to describe him as a mean son of a bitch with wit and humor as fierce as his temper. That fierce temper led to a period of estrangement when I left for college. Then, when I was twenty-eight years old, my father's anger was replaced with grief and sorrow. Yet, I watched that sorrow shrink with the birth of his grandchildren.

My dad retired and became a stay-at-home dad when my baby sister, Brit, entered kindergarten. Brit died when she was nine years old after nearly winning a valiant fight against a brain infection. She lost her life when a pharmaceutical company used a cheaper ingredient to make Heparin—a blood thinner—that ultimately caused multiple organ failure. Dad's medical problems and resulting hospitalization prevented him from paying his last respects to his youngest child. His medical insurance company stopped him from saying goodbye—they didn't feel it was medically necessary to transfer him from where he was receiving care to the hospital where his daughter was drawing her last breaths with the help of a soon-to-be-disconnected ventilator.

His cantankerous nature was washed away by the steady stream of tears that flowed for months after Brit died. During those first months, he constantly questioned why, "the good Lord took Brit and not me."

The tormenting sorrow of losing the love of his life—his reason for living—pierced a hole in his soul. He stopped yelling and started listening. After Brit died, the transformative power of grief caused my dad to realize how much energy he was wasting on his anger. When I had children, he became the most amazing grandfather to them. When no one was watching, my dad became the man he always wanted to be—he was always a man of character, but adversity taught him how to better express his feelings.

THE LOWS ARE LOWER, AND THE HIGHS DO COME

I entered parenthood already having experienced every parent's worst fear. I held the hand of my sister as her favorite nurse disconnected her from life support. The pain of living without my sister shaped me as a person and a parent.

Thirty months after we lost Brit and thirteen months after I had welcomed my firstborn (Vivian), my second daughter (Caroline) was delivered via an emergency C-section. When Caroline entered this world six weeks early, her little blue body weighed less than five pounds. This would mark the beginning of Caroline's medically complicated life.

Caroline quickly showed us she enjoys the journey as much as the destination—she does everything in her own time and on her own terms. My dad, aptly, described her as "joy personified."

Vivian made me a mother. Caroline made me a special-needs mom. Gideon, six years younger than Caroline, reminded me of the importance of rolling with the punches. Learning to mother Caroline, care for young Vivian, and work full-time was overwhelming, but somehow Caroline's medical challenges and neurological differences provided the push my dad and I needed to rebuild our relationship.

Caroline was four months old when a nurse walked into a cramped room on the pediatric floor with a stuffed bear. On that stuffed bear, my husband and I would learn how to place a nasogastric tube (NG tube), a feeding tube that entered through Caroline's nose and went to her stomach. We each practiced three times on the bear before we were given a fresh tube and coached through pushing the tube down Caroline's nose. Less than a month later, we were back at the same hospital because Caroline had become an expert at removing the NG tube.

Our only option was to have a feeding tube surgically implanted in Caroline's stomach. The surgeon would only place the gastrostomy tube (G-tube) if a Nissen Fundoplication (wrapping part of the stomach around the lower esophagus) also was performed—to minimize her GERD, which could be made worse by the G-tube. At the same time, the surgeons repaired an umbilical hernia and removed an accessory spleen discovered during surgery.

After the surgeries, Caroline stopped crying and completely stopped eating by mouth. She also started developmental, physical, speech, feeding, and occupational therapy at the ripe age of four months old. Just before her surgery, Caroline had an 80 percent developmental delay; the therapies were meant to close the gap.

SOME DOUBT THE EXISTENCE OF HEROES—THEY'VE NEVER MET MY DAD

Beyond my husband and me, my dad was the only person who felt comfortable giving Caroline a tube feed. This put him in demand even when we moved from Phoenix to Chicago to San Antonio to Cleveland Heights and finally to Cleveland; we called on him.

Less than two days before I was scheduled to start a new job in Chicago, my babysitter informed me she got a new job. No daycares would take Caroline because of her feeding tube. We needed the money and I needed to work for my sanity. I did what I'd come to always do when presented with a childcare crisis. I called my dad.

Me: "Dad, Lizzie got a job."

Dad: "That's great for Lizzie—who is she?"

Me: "The woman who watches Caroline."

Dad: "Well, that's a problem…"

He arrived in September and didn't return home until Christmas. Two other times he stayed with us for months providing free childcare because we couldn't pay anyone to care for Caroline due to her medical involvement.

At five years old, Caroline was thriving, eating food by mouth, communicating effectively using an augmentative and alternative communication device (AAC) that's like an iPad, and demonstrating her outlandish personality. I began to realize one reason my dad and Caroline connected so well: she was a female, nonverbal, autistic version of my dad.

Despite being born in the 1940s, entering the military as a teenager, guarding the Berlin Wall immediately after the assassination of President John F. Kennedy, limiting his run-ins with the law to a few nights in jail (none in prison), he found Caroline to be his new reason for living.

"She's my hero," he would proclaim after I would tell him how she stripped off her clothes and streaked through the movie theater or was caught trying to purchase airline tickets to Australia to see her favorite band, The Wiggles. Anything Caroline did was to be celebrated in my dad's eyes. And for her part, Caroline used my dad's admiration to her advantage. She learned how to call him on Alexa—she called him more than once after her dad and I told her no.

His fandom for Caroline provided me with the support I needed. My father was acting like the dad I needed him to be. To be honest, I don't think I would have given him the chance or believed it to be possible for him to change if not for Caroline's medical involvement and autism.

AUTISM CHANGED US—WE ARE DIFFERENT, STRONGER, AND MORE SELF-AWARE

We are an autism-loving family. My father's ability to move beyond accepting to a whole-hearted embracing of his grandchildren's autism is a huge part of that love. Given the choice, I would cure Caroline's epilepsy or mine and Vivian's depression. However, I would be hard-pressed to "cure" Caroline or Gideon of their autism. Yes, autism introduces unique challenges to our life, but it adds beauty and wonder.

After my dad's extended stay with us, Vivian, as a kindergartner, confidently stood in front of a microphone to introduce herself and the talent she was going to share, "My name is Vivian Buzzard and I am going to make this glass of water disappear," she said as she raised the glass above her head. After a dramatic pause, she turned around and began to slowly drink the water. The auditorium erupted in laughter. She couldn't help but peek over her shoulder before slamming back the last sip of water. When the water was finished, she spun back around and triumphantly raised the empty glass over her head, proclaiming, "I made it disappear!"

I watched it on video. My heart filled with pride before my depression allowed my guilt to transform this happy memory into a disappointing one. I closed the video and handed my husband his phone back. This was the first important event in Vivian's life that I missed—not because of Caroline's needs but because of my depression.

I had no way of knowing the decision to not attend Vivian's school's talent show would not be an isolated incident but rather would mark the beginning of a five-year struggle with severe depression, anxiety, and post-traumatic stress disorder (PTSD). Vivian was robbed of the mother she knew because I became a shell of a person. Caroline became violent and aggressive because she did not understand what was going on and I was unable to provide her with the same amount of support. Gideon and I did not bond during his infancy as I did with his sisters. I went back to work when he was two weeks old. After a few months, I learned my boss at the time brought his infant son to work with him (before I started). He did not extend the same opportunity to me. I will never know if separating from Gideon so quickly contributed to my depression, but my anger rages when I think of this injustice. And John was deprived of his wife, best friend, and co-parent. As for me, the energy that once defined me was gone. My thinking dulled, my wit muted, and my motivation to do more than survive was all but absent.

Yet, we are who we are because we choose to embrace autism rather than fight it. Our journey hasn't been easy, but it has been rewarding. Together, with my dad, we are strong enough to live this life to the fullest, to uncover the hidden joys it offers, and to laugh at things that once made us cry because autism has forced us to reevaluate the meaning of life and what we want out of it. We've redefined success, happiness, and health because of autism. Before autism entered our lives, we didn't know this was even an option. Autism taught us to control what we must, plan for what we can, and learn to embrace the unexpected.

POSTSCRIPT

As of this writing, Vivian is twelve, Caroline is eleven, and Gideon is five. All three are diagnosed with ADHD, Caroline has level 3 autism, DDX3X Syndrome (a disease caused by a spontaneous mutation within a DDX3X gene), epilepsy, and other medical involvement; Gideon has level one autism; Vivian was also diagnosed with autism in addition to diagnoses of depression and anxiety. I also was diagnosed with ADHD. Just prior to publication, after decades of declining health and increasing pain (from injuries received from a physically demanding career and his brazen ways), my dad made what was an easy decision for him: he entered hospice and passed two weeks later.

Today, Caroline communicates in full sentences using her device. In addition to attending a school for autistics, she is active in:

- **Adapted dancing with Ms. Emily of Beyond Words**. Caroline loves dancing on the big stage, especially with professional ballerinas like Ms. Elizabeth from North Pointe Ballet.

- **Music therapy.** She loves music—so much so she prefers to have people say her scripts (unique phrases or monologues that provide comfort, common for autistics) as songs.
- **Therapeutic horseback riding.** She can get her horse to stop by saying "wooo" and hold a two-point position.
- **Karate (or "karate dancing," as Caroline calls it).** She has earned a yellow belt. Occasionally, Caroline wears her pointe shoes to karate, but she always says, "boom" when punching. Mr. D keeps her on task by reminding her if she does, she will be able to break boards at the end of class.
- **Swimming.** She is working her way through Goldfish Swim School's program. She has been able to swim independently and pull herself out of water since she was six years old.
- **ABA therapy.** She is honing her powers of negotiation while learning other valuable life skills. Her goal is increasing her independence with the help of Andi and China who have been part of our journey for five years.

On tough days, Caroline loves going to Ruben's Deli where she is treated like Norm at Cheers. She has a reserved booth, her Coke and fries arrive without her having to order; frequently, she is offered the opportunity to feed melon to the pacu fish, her favorite waitress, Anna, braids her hair, and the regulars all make sure to say, "Hi."

Despite getting to know a whole new side of Caroline since she started using her device, there still are so many things about her that are enigmas. Time will provide some answers, but many will remain because part of Caroline's charming allure is the joy and beauty she finds in simple pleasures. This is not to say that Caroline is simple—quite the opposite. She knows what brings her joy and doesn't care to be bothered by things or people that fail to directly contribute to her happiness.

Before becoming a parent raising three kids at various places on the autism spectrum, I knew very little about autism. Now, I am an expert by fire. My three kids could not be more different. One has a diagnosed developmental delay; another has the IQ of a genius. What my children share are passions and strengths that define them and challenges that build their character. In a similar way, my character has been tested and strengthened by learning appropriate ways to parent each of my children to reach their unique potential and achieve their individual happiness. My children and autism have taught me the value of resilience, individuality, and humor. Autism comes with challenges but my world has been enriched by autistics.

Resource

- The best resource in the world for me is other parents who are raising kids with autism and/or medical involvement. They understand my world and can offer advice that I might be able to use. These are friends who know when to laugh, cry, or cheer. Find parents who are raising kids like yours, get to know them, and be honest with them. It will be life-changing.

Website and Blog

therapymom.co

Social Media

Facebook: therapymomkacie

Instagram: therapymomk

LinkedIn: www.linkedin.com/in/kwbuzzard

Twitter: TherapyMomK

Hashtag

#TherapyMom

My Love Letter to My Daughter, Caroline

My Dearest Caroline (Who prefers to be called Commander Catfish),

You taught me how to parent according to my heart, and you gave me the confidence I needed to become the person I am proud to be.

When I started evaluating myself based on the qualities that would help you reach your potential, I saw how my impatience was limiting me and impeding your development. You forced me to accept most things were going to take you longer to do and if I wanted you to learn to do them for yourself, I would have to be patient. Before you, I wasn't terribly understanding or flexible. You showed me there are many ways to skin a cat and more than one path to happiness.

I didn't realize it, but I started treating (most) people with the patience, kindness, and generosity I hoped the world would afford you. I smiled at strangers more, offered compliments, and was far more understanding when things didn't work out just right. These small changes introduced me to a kinder, happier world.

Despite your challenges or maybe because of them, you entered this world knowing exactly who you were, what you wanted, and how you were going to get it. Your confidence and zest for life have caused laughter and hope to replace fear and despair. You are autistic—you define autism, it doesn't define you. I love you.

BIOGRAPHY

Kacie Wielgus Buzzard is a quirky soul trying to make sense of the world and the people who surround her. Born and raised in Illinois, Kacie was never really sure where or how she fit in, mostly because she rarely does.

Kacie is a rebel—she puts ketchup on her hotdog. She is contrary, loving murder shows and chick flicks equally. And she is known for pushing the limits—too far—at least three times, the number of times she's run out of gas. Her favorite TED Talks is Andrew Solomon's "Love No Matter What," favorite philosopher is Sun Tzu, and Ruth Bader Ginsburg is her hero.

She is the founder of therapymom.co, a community for parents raising autistic kids. Kacie's a contributor on The Mighty and Kveller and she serves as a pro-bono education advocate. Kacie also works at BreezoMeter as social media manager. For twelve years, she has been (mostly happily) married to John. Together, they and their three kids: Vivian, twelve years old (autism, ADHD, depression, anxiety); Caroline, eleven years old (autism, ADHD, anxiety, DDX3X syndrome, and more); and Gideon, five years old (autism and ADHD) live in Cleveland, Ohio.

Kacie has severe depression, generalized anxiety disorder, and PTSD. For years, she has openly shared her struggles with mental health and her experiences raising three very different kids for three very different worlds. These experiences are captured on Kacie's website and social media.

A PREDESTINED JOURNEY: OUR FALL AND RISE INTO THE AUTISM WORLD

Lila Ayyad-Alharsha is a board-certified behavior analyst (BCBA), certified general and special education teacher, CEO and clinical director of Academic & Behavior Consultants of Illinois.

"Things that happen to us that may challenge us will often help us grow and have an impact on who we become."

Lucky or fortunate are not words that can describe my fall into the autism world. Predestined, meant to be, written, *Qadr* are the exact words to be used. *Qadr*, a concept from Islam, means that Allah decrees everything that happens according to his prior knowledge and wisdom. Things that happen to us that may challenge us will often help us grow and have an impact on who we become, and autism did just that. After we received the diagnosis, I thought our lives would change forever—for the worse. I couldn't have been more wrong. Instead, a whole new world opened up for me and my family!

As the youngest of four, Mustafa is the absolute love of my life! Mustafa met all of his milestones up until a little before he turned three. He was a playful child, walking by nine months and saying his first word shortly thereafter. He loved to sing! The room lit up with love when we would interact with him. Nothing he did made me seek early intervention. The only hiccups we had were chronic ear infections. I called it the year-long ear infection. From January to December, it never went away. Mustafa also had low-grade fevers that still lack explanation. I often joked at the pediatrician's office that we needed to live there. We were there so often, I was seeing them more than family. Nonetheless, the constant antibiotics were more harmful than helpful, and we decided that ear tubes would be best. That helped. The ear infections cleared and Mustafa began feeling much better.

One night, Mustafa began engaging in odd vocalizations that sounded like loud humming. I thought it was unusual, but I knew that he loved to sing, and I thought he was possibly playing with sounds. But Mustafa was slipping away slowly. As time went on, he began interacting less, stopped talking, and threw tantrums. Mustafa no longer was aware of others around him and would constantly be "on the go." My son, a bright and rambunctious little child went from being a verbal, communicative child to losing all language. I initially thought this was a phase.

My husband and I brought our concerns to the pediatrician and were referred to University of Illinois Chicago (UIC) to have Mustafa evaluated. The evaluation concluded with a diagnosis of Autism Spectrum Disorder (ASD), with the words "severe" and "nonverbal" attached. We were devastated. I asked the psychologist, "What happens next?" She responded, "There will be therapy." But no one helped us find it. It seemed as though they simply slapped on a diagnosis and moved on to the next patient. Never again did they contact us to direct us toward therapies. We were on our own! We felt taken advantage of and betrayed. Had Mustafa become just another statistic for their records? Unfortunately, no systems were in place to guide and support us. We were left grieving the "typical" child we thought we had lost.

Needless to say, I didn't know where to begin. At

the time, I was a preschool teacher and had studied early childhood development, so I understood how neurotypical children developed. However, I didn't know how to work with children with special needs.

KNOWLEDGE IS THE MOST POWERFUL TOOL

I knew I had to do something, so I searched for therapies. *He isn't speaking, so he must need speech therapy*, I thought. We contacted a clinic and once a week I would sit in their office after work until 8:30 p.m. so that Mustafa could take part in speech therapy, occupational therapy, and physical therapy. I wasn't sure what they did with him when they called him into the room.

One day, I was invited to sit in on a speech session. At first, I was upset. The therapist asked my son to sit down. I kept thinking to myself, does she not get it? *My son doesn't understand what "sit" means.* She repeated the instruction to sit. Mustafa wasn't responding. *Why did she bring me in here? To torture me? He can't do it! He doesn't understand you!* But after a few minutes, lo and behold, Mustafa sat! I was relieved but perplexed. I thought it was a fluke. She then began to ask him to place a puzzle piece onto an inset puzzle. I thought, *here we go again . . . if she asks him to do one more thing, I am going to get up, take Mustafa, and walk right out of here.* But Mustafa grabbed the piece on his own and placed it onto the puzzle! I cried!

That was my glimmer of hope. That was what I needed to see! Mustafa could learn—he just learned differently! Once I saw that Mustafa could follow these simple instructions, I thought, *well, if he can follow these two instructions, why can't he learn more!* Through that interaction, I discovered that my son could learn with a different approach. So, I decided to roll up my sleeves and start researching!

THE ABCS OF ABA

Next, I needed a support system, even if it would be hard to find. As they say, a parent of a special needs child does better research than the FBI. When I eventually found my local parent support chapter, another autism mom introduced me to Applied Behavior Analysis (ABA). I immediately began researching ABA therapy and learned that it is the gold standard for children with autism. This seemed to be exactly what we were searching for! At four-and-a-half years old, he started to receive twelve hours of ABA a week.

ABA is research-based and involves the science of behavior and learning. It helps children and adults on the spectrum increase language and communication, reduce negative behavior, and build more independent living skills. Self-help skills, such as hygiene, feeding, and dressing, are often a huge part of programming.

ABA is highly effective for everyone, not only children with autism. In fact, it is widely used and successfully applied in sports, health and fitness, criminal forensics, gerontology, organizational behavior management, and school-wide systems, such as Positive Behavioral Interventions and supports (PBIS).

Sadly, many people hear misinformation about ABA and avoid it for their child; however, those who oppose it may have been exposed to the misapplied ABA. Some may have had bad experiences with poor therapists. Nonetheless, I have witnessed many families refuse ABA, only to seek it out much later when their children were older and engaging in challenging behaviors. I encourage parents to keep an open mind and remember that early intervention is crucial. I know I am thankful to have started therapy for Mustafa early. We began to see improvements with language and communication and were excited and hopeful for the future. ABA was such a game-changer for Mustafa and can be life-changing for any child.

READY, SET, GROW

I found myself deep into the world of autism. I learned from Mustafa's therapists and applied what I learned at home. Between therapy and home, Mustafa began to make progress. He worked on many skills:

- Imitation. This helped Mustafa learn from others.
- Identifying common nouns (such as table, chair, door, toilet). This helped him understand

instructions. Later, it helped build his expressive language, so he could verbally request wants and needs.

- Identify his body parts. This helped him to express himself if something hurt.
- Dressing himself. This self-help skill helped him to build independence.

One communication strategy involved Mustafa's love of cookies. He loved cookies so much that we called him "the cookie connoisseur." He would scale the kitchen sink and comb through cabinets when we hid them. We wanted to teach him to communicate vocally, and we knew that if there was any word that he would be motivated to say it would be "cookie." So, several times, I took a cookie and cut it into small pieces. When Mustafa approached, I made the sound "C" for cookie and offer him a piece. Later, I prompted the sound "C" and waited for him to repeat it. After he repeated it, I gave him a piece. This continued with "Coo," then "Cook," then finally the full word "Cookie," where he would get the entire cookie. Mustafa finally spoke and spent his days walking up to people saying "cookie." Everyone in the house honored his request. Through this, Mustafa learned the power of his own language for the first time. Before, when he didn't know how to voice his wants and needs, he would have a tantrum or pull others to what he wanted. After, he learned that saying "cookie" was functional and required much less effort than a tantrum. From here, we continued to teach him new words and expand to sentences and social communication.

FINDING YOUR PURPOSE

As a parent, I continued to use what I learned with Mustafa. In addition, I started to find that some of the treatments I used with my son worked in my classroom. I was intrigued by how effective ABA was in my work and life. I also wanted to contribute to changing the mindset of educators and administrators in regard to inclusion for children with special needs. So, I decided to go back to school, study school administration, complete certification as a behavior analyst, and practice ABA.

The next chapter of my life as a parent and professional changed. Mustafa was settled and beginning to progress, but as a teacher and a parent, I found myself always fighting for inclusive opportunities. Our children were viewed as if they were separate from the classroom, not the responsibility of the general education teacher. As if they didn't belong.

Because of this, I left teaching after seventeen and a half years and moved into an administrative role as assistant principal in hopes of changing mindsets. I continued to advocate for the special-needs population and, after completing my BCBA, I yearned for more. I wanted to help other families like mine and let them know the possibilities.

To pursue this purpose, I accepted a position as the director of education for a Helping Hand School, a therapeutic day school that reaches over thirty-three districts in Illinois. This school served families and children that had needs that exceeded what school districts could offer. Guiding both staff and families became my passion! I also began assisting families as a BCBA outside of my full-time job as an administrator. As their children began to make great progress, the families began referring other families to me. I eventually started my own ABA company, Academic & Behavior Consultants of Illinois, also known as ABC Health, where I continue to serve families and provide them with access to quality programming. I have the honor and privilege of being a source of guidance and relief for families that have struggled. I found my purpose through my son and am grateful that God granted me the means to support others.

THE BLESSING WITHIN

When difficult things happen, it may instead turn out to be good for us, just what we needed, for Allah knows best. When Mustafa was first diagnosed, I had so much difficulty, yet my husband, a devout Muslim, immediately accepted it. My husband was more religious than I had been and understood the significance of having a child with special needs, that God had given us a great opportunity through his grace and mercy to be rewarded with heaven through loving and caring for our beautiful child. I became more religious and established a deeper connection with Allah.

Through this journey, I came to understand *Qadr* and the significance of autism in our lives. So many blessings came from the autism world. It allowed me to serve families in need and brought me closer to Allah, connecting me to our creator in a way that I could have never imagined. We have placed our faith in Allah, comforted that he is the sustainer and protector. We rely solely on him. Difficulty made me seek him more often and my focus in life changed.

In turn, Mustafa taught us all about compassion for others, patience, love, kindness, and respect for all. He taught us that everyone is different in their own special way and that, God-willing, anything is possible. Mustafa's diagnosis put life into perspective!

At seventeen years old, Mustafa continued to make great progress. He is very independent and effectively communicates his wants and needs with us. Our ultimate goal has always been to help Mustafa live an optimal life as we continue building communication and independent living skills. He truly is our blessing, our gift, and he has taught us more about life and what matters most! With his diagnosis, I had suspected that our lives were going to change forever. I was right—and what a spectacular change it was!

Reflection

1. What challenges have come your way that you thought would take you down but have only made you stronger?
2. How has your child taught you life lessons and redirected you to what matters most?
3. Knowledge is power: What will you do next to arm yourself with the tools you need to help your child make continuous progress?

Resources

- The Verbal Behavior Approach by Mary Lynch Barbera
- Let Me Hear Your Voice by Catherine Maurice
- Autism Speaks
- The Turn Autism Around podcast

Social Media
Facebook: ABCHealthAutismTherapy
Instagram: ABCHealthTherapy

Hashtags
#TheBlessingWithin #KnowledgeIsPower
#FindingYourPurpose #BCBAMom
#ABARocks #ChallengesMakeYouStronger

Love Letter to Autism

Dear Autism,

You came into our lives, and we had thought you had swept our child away only to find out that you came to help us understand the true meaning of life, its rewards, and tests, and what is most important.

You challenged us in ways that we never thought possible.

You challenged us to fight ignorance and superstition, to educate and advocate for others, and to prove that our children can and will!

You challenged us to become compassionate and patient and taught us to give the benefit of the doubt, and to love everyone!

You taught us to rely on our Creator, especially as we put our heads down on our pillows every night, as we wonder what will happen to our children when we are no longer here.

You taught us to serve others and to see the blessings and beauty in everything.

You taught us to celebrate every milestone met and every success had and to cherish the innocence of our beautiful children. If every human being was as pure as our children, our world would be a much different and better place!

Lila Ayyad-Alharsha MEd, BCBA

As for you, Mustafa, if you only knew how much we love you and cherish the privilege God has granted us as your parents. You are our blessing!

We are blessed to have you in our lives and are thankful for the challenges that made us better human beings!

With love and complete admiration!

Mom

BIOGRAPHY

Lila Ayyad-Alharsha MEd, BCBA, has over twenty-five years of educational and professional experience in both the general and Special Education settings. She is a board-certified behavior analyst (BCBA) and a certified general and special education teacher. Lila holds a master's degree in educational leadership along with a bachelor's degree in early childhood education. Lila is the CEO and clinical director of Academic & Behavior Consultants of Illinois, also known as ABC Health, which works towards transforming the lives of families by providing quality ABA in-home and clinic-based services. Lila began her career as a teacher and also served as an assistant principal at Harnew Elementary in Oak Lawn, Illinois. For six years, Lila also served as the director of education for Helping Hand School in Countryside, Illinois, a therapeutic day school serving children diagnosed with autism.

Lila was recognized as Teacher of the Year in 2003 and was nominated for a Golden Apple Award in 2005. Lila has conducted trainings for educators, parents, youth leaders, and supervisors, and she also provides school consultative services for teachers and students struggling in classrooms. Lila and her husband, Naser, reside in Palos Heights, Illinois, with their four children Nisreen, Bilal, Mohammad, and Mustafa. Her youngest child, Mustafa (diagnosed with autism), is the blessing of her life, and Lila works to educate and advocate for others through her experience as a parent, educator, and BCBA.

AUTISM SURE IS FUNNY

Hugo Morales is a first-time author, father to an autistic boy, a John Maxwell Certified Instructor, volunteer extraordinaire for The Autism Hero Project, and a sales and tech enthusiast. You can connect with him via email, LinkedIn, Twitter, and Instagram.

"Live so that when your children think of love, fairness, integrity, and tenderness, they think of you."
–H. Jackson Brown, Jr.

To understand how I feel about raising a young man who's on the spectrum, I'd have to start with telling you about me. I was raised by my biological uncle and his wife, but I grew up blocks away from my biological mother and her own family. While I lived with my uncle, aunt, and four cousins, I broke bread, went on trips, celebrated events, exchanged gifts, and even fought with my mom's three other kids—my brothers and sister. We did regular family things but with a twist: I never stayed. I had to watch the clock or else walk home in the dark alone. When I was younger, I tried to explain my family's dynamic, but it was complicated. No matter whose house I was at, I had a different last name. It raised questions. Was I adopted? Was I the milkman's kid? I didn't know exactly where I fit in, but I simply accepted it. As if I didn't really have a choice. I wasn't trying to change the situation, I just wanted to understand it. Splitting myself between two families became my norm. Whatever you're a part of, your tribe, however you grew up, that's the norm, your norm. This prepared me for what was to come.

My norm changed on July 19, 2010, when Maximillian came into our lives. I like to say he's my "second firstborn" because my sons are nearly sixteen years apart. Maximillian's birth was a new experience all over again. I was hoping that I had learned all I needed from having his older brother, Sebastian. At the least, I thought we had learned what not to do. But watching the birth of Maxim was nothing like Sebastian's. It was a struggle from the start. My family was at the hospital. They flew in to help us with the new little wonder about to enter our lives. As we were waiting in the delivery room, a nurse abruptly came in. She asked us to move out of the way and for my family to exit.

My beautiful wife, Tamika, was shifted on the delivery bed, lights and sounds changed like an airplane cockpit—when the plane's going down. Panic set in. I didn't know why; I just knew the signs weren't good. After struggle, lights, beeping, heavy breathing, and serious pushing, my boy was born, blue as a newborn Smurf with the umbilical cord wrapped around his neck. The cord was cut, his vitals were checked, and we watched in shock as he sat under a heat lamp. After an hour, he was finally ready for us and the world.

HIS NAME IS MAXIM

We brought my little man home. Early on, we settled on the nickname Maxim, as the conversations of "no one is allowed to call him Max because they're too lazy to fully pronounce his name" started. Also, for the record, the first few times someone said, "How's Max doing?" or anything with "Max," Tamika met it quickly with, "His name is Maximillian. You can call him Maxim but not Max," followed with a look of death. As time went on, it was tough to keep up with everyone calling him Max, so it *kind of* got accepted. But once in a while, Tamika's look of death comes out from left field, and I laugh inside.

A few years passed, and Maxim grew into a child that loved to have fun, run, laugh, and play all the time. He was the life of the party. Maxim had so much energy—the Energizer Bunny would retire because of him! He was growing into this face worthy of—dare I say—TV ads. People were enamored by how beautiful he was. So beautiful that in public we'd be stopped by other mothers who would say, "She's beautiful!" Of course, we would correct them by saying "She's a he" and "thank you." This was always followed up by, "Well, he's so gorgeous that he could be a girl," which somehow was supposed to be better. Many times, I wanted to make a T-shirt for him that said, "Look down, I have a penis," so that I wouldn't have to correct others. Maxim had a face and cheeks that were so chubby that I gave him a second nickname, Bubba. You know the friend we all had that looked like he was smuggling bags of nuts in his mouth like a chipmunk? Mom couldn't keep up with the demand of that little sucker.

PIZZA ME THIS...

Maxim was getting taller and cuter right before our eyes, and it was fun to watch. He wanted to play all the time, probably too much—even if it was 7 a.m. We'd be at parties, and he was constantly running everywhere nonstop. He just had to keep going. If pushed, he would parallel play, play side by side with kids, but most times, he was happy by himself. Any social gathering we brought him to, he was the only kid playing in the corner. Also, when it came to food, he only wanted to eat anything with a crispy texture. The good stuff: chips, crackers, and eventually pizza. It was getting tougher to feed him. He didn't want to eat the greens or fruits. Our joy slowly changed into being worried for his health as it became more difficult for us to make progress on what we could get him to eat.

We made different choices raising Sebastian. Then, we were young parents and inexperienced. Because of this, we chose to raise Maxim a little differently: no meat, more greens, and healthier foods, especially since Tamika and I were mostly vegetarian. But the problem persisted. Maxim did not want to eat the "healthy things." He wasn't eating what we wanted. Worse, he really only ate a handful of things, and none of it was *bueno*.

Then, one day, as I was heading home, I ordered a large cheese pizza from Giordano's. The second I made my way up the stairs, Maxim was already waiting at the top step for me as he usually did. Nothing made me feel more at home than this—he was always excited to see me and would jump up and down.

I slowly opened the box of pizza and Maxim was staring at me funny with his head sideways, the way my dog looks at me at times. I separated a slice, removed the cheese, and ran my finger deep into the tomato sauce, rubbing all of it on my finger. Then I just jammed it into his mouth for him to try. He stepped back with suspicion and began to smack his lips a few times. Then BOOM! It was like we found the famous missing Japanese sword Honjo

Masumune. Maxim liked it, and we hit another stride that day. Tamika was quick to remind me that he can't live off pizza alone. I thought, *why not?*

YIN AND YANG

Tamika and I have different roles with Maxim. He is still a very selective eater, so I get up early to cook him breakfast before school and make him a hot lunch of his favorite foods to take with him. Meanwhile, Tamika is the one who likes to bark orders and make sure that I am including blueberries with his chicken nuggets or cucumbers with his pizza bites. I take Maxim to karate and talk Pokèmon with him. Tamika is the one who works with him on school assignments and with the therapists. Out of both of us, she tends to worry more about his future, and how he will be treated, respected, and included. She thinks about his independence and turns everything into lessons on life skills. She thinks more intentionally and rightfully so. I, on the other hand, am probably a little too laid back. Our personalities are very much shaped by our life experiences and because of that—we are truly yin and yang.

Even the day we received the diagnosis we were unalike in our reactions. I didn't flinch and just thought we would figure this out by tomorrow. Tamika thought about what his diagnosis could mean for his future. It's no wonder that she took Maxim's diagnosis hard. So hard that she forbade me from sharing his diagnosis with anyone, not even our family. As time went on, I started to feel differently about not telling family, but I knew she wasn't ready to share yet. She was still grieving. And I'm not sure why I never really grieved Maxim's diagnosis, but I think it was because Maxim was such a happy child. Yes, he was slower at meeting his milestones and they didn't come easy, but he eventually met them. All in his time. Maxim was practically five when he was diagnosed and, by that time, he was already reading and nearly potty trained. The only thing that was different to me after that day was that there was an explanation for his behaviors. So, I didn't feel the need to grieve. He was always laughing and singing. I didn't know that much about autism, but I knew about Maxim.

A year later, we planned to visit our families. I had decided to tell my family and swear them to secrecy. In my mind, they needed to know. I also wanted to ensure that they understood what being on the spectrum means. They didn't know much about autism. I explained to the best of my ability how being autistic could affect Maxim and us. My sister Marge, who usually gets things quickly, understood and after our conversation, simply replied, "Whatever you need, Hugo." I asked them to do some research, spend time with him, and more importantly, let him be himself. And they have done exactly that. They love Maxim and accept him for who he is, and I feel blessed to have such a loving and supporting family. I just regret that we live in different states, but they love him as unconditionally as we do.

LAUGH LINES AND WRINKLES

One day we were repeatedly calling out to Maximillian, and he was not responding. My wife asked him, "Did you not hear us calling you?" The next thing I know, Maxim was declaring a name change. He now wanted to be referred to as "The Legendary Kid." Tamika gave me a look as if to say, we're going to entertain this idea. She then argued that it was longer than his real name and insisted that he needed a nickname. After some back and forth, we settled on calling him "Legend" for short.

This is one example of how Maximillian is great for random, funny stuff. The many laughs that Maxim has provided with his own black-and-white approach have been endless. I've lost track of how many times I've blown snot laughing in front of adults at what he's done or said—things I definitely shouldn't have laughed at. Once in karate class, Maxim's sensei stood in front of him and asked, "How are you doing?" Maxim held his nose and flapped his hand as he said, "Your breath stinks." I was embarrassed and told Maxim that he couldn't say things like that. Only for him to respond, "But, it's true. His breath does stink."

Another time, we were out to breakfast before school,

and I asked the waitress for a refill on my coffee. When she returned, Maxim went knuckle-deep into his pants. Horrified, I said, "What are you doing right now!?" Maxim with a straight face and without hesitation said, "I'm scratching my nuts like you do." The waitress laughed so hard she cried and spilled coffee on the table. Most parents would have turned a few shades of red, but I smirked and said to myself, *that's my boy!* Then, of course, I had to explain why doing that was inappropriate.

If there is anything that you can take away from these stories, it's to give yourself permission to be in the moment and laugh. Laugh so hard that those wrinkles shine through. We're all heading to the same place, so you might as well go with laughter lines and wrinkles. Earn them along the way by living in the joy of those who can say things that you probably wish you could say.

What I've learned from my little man is that, no matter how hard it gets, you must find the humor, cherish and revel in the moments that you can laugh at. When we dwell on the worst, it consumes the silver lining.

Be present, share stories, take photos and videos, journal, blog or keep a diary, because documenting will help keep the memories alive. Facebook Memories are the best because you can live that memory all over again. We love to record videos and Tamika is always using social media to share our stories, to raise awareness, and to be a resource for others. We also love to share the awkward, odd, and crazy moments to help our community laugh a little more or gain insight that will help fuel acceptance. When you change your mindset, moments like these help you realize the progress that your child makes, the learning, the growing, and the constant resilience.

Our energy, body language, and tone tell our children how we feel. In the end, "You should live so that when your children think of love, fairness, integrity, and tenderness, they think of you." As Maxim has grown, I've embraced our new norm—my hope, my want, and my desire are that other families do the same.

Resource
- AutismHeroProject.org

Social Media
Instagram: hugoboss1170
LinkedIn: www.linkedin.com/in/hugomorales11

Hashtag
#AutismIsFunny

Love Letter to My Son

Dear Maxim,

As I lie on my bed every night unwinding from the long day of adulting, I watch you walk past my bedroom. You're on your way to bed after your daily reminder to brush your teeth and call it a night. I ask, "Hey, dude, where's my hug!?"

As you jump onto my bed, we embrace in a long silent hug, and I massage your back. You sit closer to my chest as I tighten my hug. I rub your head, massaging and tickling you—you squirm in my arms, and I try to hold you down.

What you don't realize, Maxim, is that I'm trying to rub away and shield you from what this world does not understand about you. I see people's reactions and the looks of other adults when we go out in public. They don't see you the way I do, my love. They judge you, or they judge me by your behavior or things that you may say and do. Most don't understand your mind nor your heart, what may run through it, the things that you say. Hell, at times I don't know myself, but guess what? I love it because that's you! But more importantly, the joy that I get watching you come into my bedroom, kissing me and squeezing me hard saying, "I love you and goodnight," is also the same way you wake up every morning—a cycle of joy.

Know this, my son: wherever you decide to take your life and what you want to accomplish, your mother and I will be there every step of the way.

Love,

Papi

BIOGRAPHY

Hugo Morales is a sales executive, customer service guru, and entrepreneur. He has spent nearly thirty years in the telecommunications industry working with people all over the country. The most rewarding parts of his career have been the opportunities to coach, groom, and work with some of the best salespeople in the industry.

When he's not working, Hugo enjoys time with his two boys, Sebastian and Maximillian, and his beautiful wife, Tamika. He loves traveling, sports, comedy, and all things New England! Hugo has a heart for the homeless and has volunteered for more than a decade in serving the homeless. His other passions include raising awareness and acceptance for autism. You can always find Hugo behind the scenes at all the events for The Autism Hero Project (AHP). Whether it's the heavy lifting, driving, setting up, or "honey, do this," he's the man!

3,122 DAYS

Marc Mar-Yohana, founder and CEO of OtisHealth, passionate healthcare advocate, technology enthusiast, and builder.

"May parents cherish and celebrate every moment."

I had eight years, six months, and sixteen days with my daughter, Constance, before she passed away. She died of a brain tumor. She was never diagnosed. The type of cancer that claimed her life is incurable, even when diagnosed early. Her symptoms, painful as they were, were masked by her inability to talk and show pain as a neurotypical child would. Constance's death brought my wife and me to our knees and ultimately claimed our marriage.

This story ends with a tragedy, one that no parent should ever have to face.

Yet, I still have a wonderful and hopeful story to share, marked by the days of our little girl's heartbreaking struggles and amazing triumphs. May some parents find this story helpful in their autism journey. Most importantly, may parents cherish and celebrate every moment with their children.

DAY 1: ELATION, EXCITEMENT, AND COMMITMENT

When we have a child, most of us think about what we are going to teach them, how we are going to provide for them, how we will be there for them. From the time that little fragile life enters the world, we are suddenly focused, elated, and terrified. I am sure not everyone feels like this. This is how I felt. I knew I was going to be the best dad I could be. What I didn't know was how much my little girl was going to teach me.

DAY 730: EVERY DAY IS A FUN DADDY-DAUGHTER ADVENTURE

The first two years of Constance's life were like many children's lives. She needed regular diaper changes, she hit all the benchmarks for growth and health, she laughed, and she nuzzled. She was always so happy to see her mother and me. It seemed everyone we met wanted to hold her and offered to babysit. Parents asked for baby dates. Even the baristas at the local Starbucks would get excited to see Constance exploring the coffee shop, giggling and smiling at everyone. Our little girl was the center of our lives and firmly defined who I always wanted to be: her dad.

DAY 1,096: AUTISM! WHAT DOES THAT MEAN? IS THERE A CURE?

After Constance turned two years old and before she turned three years old, we saw a change. She stopped making eye contact. The few words she knew disappeared. She struggled to talk. She would grab our mouths as we spoke in what seemed to be a desperate attempt to mimic our facial movements. She sat in front of the mirror, by herself, pushing her cheeks and trying to mouth words. Nothing would come out but tones and grunts.

We went to parks together. Children would run up to her to get her to play with them. When she was unable to respond, they would quickly abandon her and run to play with other children. The hardest moment for me was to watch her cry, holding her face in her hands, when she saw other children playing and realized that they wouldn't play with her.

Our daughter was diagnosed with autism and apraxia of speech. These two conditions effectively muted her to the regular, speaking world. They also caused physical coordination issues. Though she had been walking for some time, she had trouble with balance. When we spoke to her, it wasn't clear what, if anything, she understood.

I was so angry. Where did we screw up? Did someone else screw up? How could we fix this?

We thought we did everything right. We had been obsessive about anything that could have affected her health. She had the best prenatal and early childhood medical care. Nearly everything she ate was organic. We had tested the house for chemicals. We had used low-VOC paint in her bedroom. She had all-natural bedding and clothing.

We had no answers.

DAY 1,461: AUTISM PARENTS TO THE RESCUE!

For nearly a year, Constance endured weekly visits with specialists, had clinical assessments, cognitive studies, and therapeutic interventions. We tried nearly every available medical treatment to cure Constance, including chelation treatments to remove toxic metals and even a stem cell transplant. It was so upsetting to force Constance to have her blood drawn or her skin pricked countless times. So many people claimed that children had been cured. Nothing we tried seemed to help.

Medical professionals advised us to make plans for our daughter to be institutionalized. We were shocked! There was no way we were giving up on our child and locking her up in a facility.

In our drive to find answers, we met many other parents of children with autism. They became our best source of information and advice. Autism parents dove into action at any request for help. They were a tight-knit and giving community that often made substantial sacrifices to provide the best care for their children. We quickly learned about the importance of Applied Behavior Analysis (ABA) therapy, the best therapists and doctors to see, which treatments worked, the limitations of medical insurance, and how to plan for the long run.

We were finally getting answers. We also made an important realization:

We needed to stop looking for a cure and focus on our daughter's immediate health needs, her strengths, her education, and her happiness.

My wife purchased books and videos on sign language. She taught Constance how to sign. Soon our little girl was talking to us again and she was happy.

My wife also found a fantastic private preschool called Cherry Preschool in Evanston, Illinois. They have an inclusion program where children with special needs are in the same classroom as all other children. They are each assigned an aid to help them with the lessons and participation. She was finally able to make friends and play. Constance loved Cherry Preschool.

DAY 1,826: EVERYTHING IS SO EXPENSIVE

Eventually Constance outgrew Cherry Preschool and we enrolled her in regular classes at a local public school. The public-school programs forced all children to follow identical regimens. Little was catered to Constance's learning style and cognitive limitations. As a simple example, a school evaluator said Constance didn't know or regularly forgot basic words like "elephant," and forced her to repeat the elephant lesson daily. We had to explain that she had known what an elephant was since she was one. It just took her a long time to respond to, "What is this a picture of?" with the verbal answer, "elephant." The public-school teachers didn't believe us. It was infuriating! It also visibly distressed Constance to be at this school. We pulled her out after a few weeks.

Constance needed a different educational approach. She had the most success learning during her ABA therapy sessions, which she had been receiving for a year. Now that she was out of Cherry Preschool, she began receiving forty hours of ABA therapy a week. It was intensive and incredibly expensive. Yet it clearly was making a difference. She was able to speak a few phrases more regularly. She would read out loud. We also noticed something even more remarkable. Constance was happy in therapy. She would motivate herself in her therapy sessions, and she loved the new skills she was learning. Her therapists even commented how Constance would pull them back to their practice table from breaks early so she could try the next task.

ABA therapy was working for Constance. She stopped signing and began pushing herself to talk, asking for things and answering questions verbally. It was extraordinary. We were so proud of her.

I mentioned that ABA was expensive. When Constance first started receiving ABA therapy, medical insurance companies covered little, and our out-of-pocket expenses were astronomical. With the passage of the Affordable Care Act and some changes to medical insurers' policies regarding ABA therapy, we were able to get more of her sessions covered. However, the co-payments were still hundreds of dollars a week. We cut many personal expenses to cover these costs and went into debt.

About this time, we realized something frightening. Our little girl would require a lifetime of healthcare and would probably never be able to support herself. We needed to save enough money, not just for our retirement, but also for Constance's entire life. How does anyone do this?

Amid this realization, I lost my job.

I was horrified at the prospect of being unable to support Constance's care. She was making great progress and we needed my income. Nothing in my life has motivated me like being Constance's dad. I saw how hard she worked every day with her therapists. I saw her practice her new skills even when she thought no one was looking. I needed to be as tough and driven as she was.

I quickly went to work finding a new job. While looking, I took short-term gigs as a consultant. I was fortunate that my wife was still employed and the short-term consulting work paid well. Even so, we had to use debt to carry us to the next year. We were starting to become desperate. Although I had received several offers for full-time work, I convinced my wife we needed to hold out a little longer. I knew our longer-term financial needs and waited for an opportunity that would meet them.

DAY 2,191: WHO WILL LOVE CONSTANCE WHEN WE ARE GONE?

We seemed to be on the right path now. I found a great job. We could take care of all of Constance's care and start planning for her future. Part of that planning included signing her up for government disability support services so she would receive assistance after we passed away.

It is so strange to plan for our eventual passing that early. We had been so focused on providing for her and supporting her that we hadn't been able to have other children. Constance has no siblings. Who would look out for her or simply check on her to make sure she's OK? Where would she live? Who will love Constance when we are gone?

I can say at this point in our autism journey that I really began to understand more about children and adults with autism. We had heard that Autism Spectrum Disorder (ASD) takes many forms. We met folks from across the spectrum. One of the most rewarding and eye-opening volunteer work experiences was with Aspiritech, a company in the Chicago area that employs adults with autism to conduct software and system testing. The wonderful founders, Moshe and Brenda Weitzberg, have a son on the spectrum. They created this company to help him find meaningful work. Over ten years it will have grown to an organization that employs over 120 full-time staff with more than 90 percent on the spectrum. My wife and I volunteered with them for many of those years. In working with the Weitzbergs and the staff, I learned that adults with autism have aspirations, were driven to grow, and, with some basic accommodations, could be successful. The employees were a happy, supportive community. They worked together and helped each other. Aspiritech gave us hope that one day Constance would belong to a community. She would have friends and people that would care about her. She would have a life after us.

DAY 2,557: BEING AN ADVOCATE

At every chance, I took Constance on adventures: miniature golf, the botanical garden, the woods, the beach, the park. She had become great at climbing playground equipment and loved playing Mario Kart and golf on her Wii. Constance also received a special friend and protector that year, Otis, her service dog. They went everywhere together and were quite the pair. All the locals at stores and restaurants recognized them. She was known in our community.

My wife and I also became good at being Constance's advocate. Once we were on the beach with Otis and a park district manager demanded we leave the beach unless we produced a document proving that Otis was a service dog. We knew the law and told him he was wrong to tell us to leave. We gave him a copy of a pamphlet published by the Justice Department explaining Constance's rights with the service dog. He threatened to call the police. We stood our ground. No one was going to bully our daughter. He called the police. The police arrived and lectured the man and his supervisor on the law. We were not kicked off the beach and the park district staff apologized.

To be clear, we were extraordinarily angry. But being angry wasn't going to help. Most of the general public does not know about autism and the rights of people with disabilities. We knew a big part of our role in advocating for Constance was to educate people . . . again and again and again.

DAY 2,922: MANY MEDICAL NEEDS

Constance had a major seizure in January of 2017. On top of autism and being unable to speak like a typical child, she was now diagnosed with epilepsy. How can life be so cruel! She worked so hard. Why couldn't she get a break?

Despite all the focus on autism, our child still had many other medical needs. She saw a dentist every six months, but it took a long time to find one that would listen to us. Some dentists said they would see Constance but would only work on her teeth if she was sedated or anesthetized (knocked out). Ridiculous! We finally found one dental office that did listen, and we trained the dental hygienists on how to talk with Constance and clean her teeth. It was simple. Tell Constance what you are going to do and ask her permission to do it. When she opens her mouth, it's OK to proceed. When she pushes your hand away, she needs a break. They followed the instructions perfectly. Constance never cried, was never upset, and was never afraid to be at the dentist's office.

Now that our daughter was diagnosed with epilepsy, we had an additional group of specialists to see. We carefully picked her new care team, walking away from anyone that rushed us or was annoyed by our questions. Most importantly, the care team we selected spoke to Constance directly and listened to her.

DAY 3,111: CONSTANCE'S LAST WEEK

In March of 2018, we went to Disney World, thanks to Constance's grandparents. She loved everything Disney, saw the Lion King show, met Goofy, Minnie Mouse, Princess Merida, and Rapunzel, and had so much fun on the rides. Four days after our return, Constance collapsed.

We didn't know Constance had cancer. We were with her every day and didn't see it. Her therapists missed it. Her neurologist missed it. Her last MRI showed nothing.

As the neurosurgeon explained Constance had an inoperable brain tumor, I was sure he was talking about another child. He was talking about Constance. They were unable to save her.

Constance had been in horrific pain, and we had been unaware. Her difficulty speaking and expressing herself hid the symptoms from us. All the professionals and our friends said we couldn't have known. I felt I had failed her. My life meant nothing without her . . . no mission . . . nothing to love.

As time passes, I reflect on those 3,122 days with her. We had many special moments and memories with Constance, and I know we did the best we could for our little girl. We learned early on with Constance that we needed to find fun wherever and whenever we could. How fortunate we were that her last week with us was filled with joy.

I still miss her.

Resources
- Cherry Preschool: cherrypreschool.org
- Aspiritech: aspiritech.org
- Autism Service Dogs of America: autismservicedogsofamerica.org
- The Autism Hero Project: autismheroproject.org

Website: otishealth.net

Social Media
Facebook: otishealth

LinkedIn: otishealth

Facebook: marc mar-yohana

LinkedIn: marc mar-yohana

Hashtag
#CelebrateYourChild

My Love Letter to Constance

My Dearest Little Girl,

I am so proud of you. You worked so hard and never gave up. You knew you were different and not everyone was nice to you. Yet you pushed ahead and showed us all how to have fun. From your giggles, to your endless desire to jump, to our wonderful walks in the forest, we have so many wonderful memories.

I learned so much from you: how to be patient, how to love, and how to give big hugs. I learned that for some, simple tasks can be difficult at first, but with a change of perspective, they can succeed. I learned that everyone has a voice and sometimes needs help to be heard.

The most important thing I learned from you was how to be a dad. You inspired me to work harder and push myself, just like you pushed yourself every day. Because of our time together, I am rededicating my life to help others. Whenever I am unsure if I can do something, I think of you, smile, and then get back to work. I hope one day I make you proud, too.

I love you Constance and miss you very much.

Love,
Dad

BIOGRAPHY

Marc Mar-Yohana founded OtisHealth in honor of his late daughter, Constance. OtisHealth is named after Constance's service dog, Otis, a faithful companion and constant protector. The mission of OtisHealth is to empower people with personalized insights to improve their health, the health of their loved ones, and lives in their community. This includes implementing artificial intelligence (AI) systems to help actively manage health and provide early disease detection. In his personal outreach, Marc brings together members of the medical, AI, and advocacy communities to solve issues in personal health management and healthcare equity.

Prior to OtisHealth, Marc held executive leadership roles in investment management at safety science company, UL, and private equity firm, Pfingsten Partners; principal strategic consulting roles at NTT Data, M Operations, and Zerinc Technologies; and engineering and operations leadership roles with Emerson Electric and Honeywell Aerospace.

Marc holds a bachelor's degree in mechanical engineering from Northern Illinois University and a master's in Business Administration from Arizona State University. He completed an executive leadership program at Yale University as well as Artificial Intelligence and Machine Learning coursework at Massachusetts Institute of Technology and Stanford University.

Marc served as an adjunct professor of graduate studies at Saint Xavier University, teaching courses in global marketing, consumer behavior, and international business. He is a member of Healthcare Information Management Systems Society (HIMSS) and the Association of Clinical Research Professionals (ACRP). He is also an industry advisor for Valley Machine Learning and Artificial Intelligence (ValleyML.ai) and the conference program chair for AI Expo 2021.

A MOTHER'S PROMISE

Belqui Ortiz-Millili is the founder of Bella Vida for Autism Mothers, where she specializes in autism support coaching. She is also the founder and chef at Belqui's Twist, a culinary blog dedicated to Latin Caribbean cooking and Latin Fusion recipes. As a recurring contributor on cooking TV segments, she has been featured in Panasonic, Walmart+, and other campaigns. You can connect with her on Instagram and LinkedIn.

"My promise of love strengthens me along the way."

Autism. Heard or seen, a word of many emotions, many experiences.

I have been an autism mom for twelve years and have learned to appreciate the good, the bad, and the ugly.

I had triplets prematurely at twenty-seven weeks. Only two of the three were born alive—Connor and Natalie. Then, five days later, both experienced brain bleeds. Connor's was only a minor bleed, but Natalie's was severe. We had to say goodbye. I held her during her passing, and promised, as I kissed her face over and over again, that I would care for her brother. I would love him unconditionally.

My son on the spectrum, Connor, was the sole survivor.

The months that followed, I grieved every day for my baby girl. I saw Connor and imagined her next to him, smiling, giggling, or just existing. Those were jabs to the heart many times a day.

Connor was a colicky baby and that lasted five months, a very loooong five months. But every time I was upset, I reminded myself of my promise to Natalie and changed my disposition immediately to come from a place of love and compassion. Little did I know this was only the beginning of how my promise would be tested.

At thirteen months, Connor's development was unlike his older brother Evan's. He wasn't as attentive or engaged as before. He stopped waving bye-bye. He still laughed a lot and smiled but sometimes it was at absolutely nothing.

He would be doing it all by himself like he had inside jokes. I brought up these concerns to his pediatrician and was told this was normal for preemies and boys. "They just don't develop as fast as girls." That didn't sit well. My intuition told me that something was different, off. By eighteen months, I was told that he was developmentally delayed. That he needed therapy. My intuition had been right—I knew my child well.

At this point, I had told the pediatrician that I suspected he had autism. I saw all the signs. During my first pregnancy, I had read books on many motherhood topics because I wanted to be prepared for anything that came my way.

At twenty-one months, after several evaluations, Connor was finally diagnosed with autism. Unbelievably, I was elated! I could finally help my son! I ran out of that specialist's office and immediately started making phone calls. I was so busy making sure I got him the help he needed, I couldn't feel anything else but intense focus for several days. Then I finished setting up the last of four appointments for his evaluations. That was when the sorrow hit me: he's almost two years old, not saying a single word, not walking, not making real eye contact. I began to cry almost every day, wondering what the future held for him.

Soon therapists began to come and go all day from our home. As an overachiever, I organized a lot of therapy.

Applied Behavior Analysis (ABA) alone was twenty-five hours a week. Speech, occupational, physical, and feeding therapies rounded up to thirty-five hours. I was feeling wonderful about his possibilities watching these amazing therapists.

During that time, I learned so much from having therapists in our home. I learned how to incorporate therapy into everyday life. How to phrase things when speaking to him. Even Evan, three years old at the time, started applying the tools he saw at home. We had him participate in some sessions and sometimes Evan was better at following through than my husband and I were. Evan called us out when we didn't use the right wording with Connor. We loved it! To this day Evan is great at making sure we do everything as we should.

As a parent whose child was diagnosed so early, I am a big proponent of therapies at home at that age. That way, the therapy is in their environment. I also find it helpful to involve other children, if you have them, because they can be part of learning their sibling's needs. One big challenge we faced as a family was my husband's constant traveling at the time. When he returned home from his business trips, he had to be filled in on every single development in Connor's therapies. If there was a new way to word something, new ways to get him to eat something, to ask for something, to do something, etc. It sounds easy but for me it was exhausting because I also had to make sure he was following through properly.

Eventually, Connor started school at three years old. This was an amazing experience for us. Mainly because we could incorporate much-needed socialization with other children. He did, though, stay much to himself. He played side-by-side with other kids but not with them— parallel play. But aside from that, this early age was great for us. We had some trepidation as we handed him over to teachers and paraprofessionals that we did not know. Why? Because he was nonverbal, he couldn't tell us anything about his days there. But soon these people became like family. We were absolutely blessed to be in a great school district.

Now that he was in school full-time, his at-home therapies were lowered to once a week for each, except ABA two to three times a week. We managed well with this change, and I got to have a break, which was wonderful. I now was able to do more for myself. I began to study for a life coaching certification. I wanted to help moms like myself navigate the autism journey, especially addressing the emotions that come right after diagnosis. These emotions can be crippling and I wanted to know exactly how to guide them to act and to help their child instead of feeling paralyzed. Once I achieved this certification, I worked to share my knowledge in a non-profit setting. This was free to the moms I worked with.

THE UGLY YEARS

Between ages three and six, Connor wasn't potty trained, and he just didn't get it. He didn't understand what poop was and would take his diaper off and smear. He had this down to a T! Sometimes, he did great works of art with it. You can imagine the challenge. Somehow, I handled it with patience and found ways to avoid accidents by dressing him in one-piece pajamas with a zippered back, or jumpsuits and even overalls. I swear by them now—these are a must for parents.

At this age, we also dealt with a lot of meltdowns and self-harm. These, I believe, are the hardest part of dealing with his autism. Our family does, to this day, the best we can to make Connor's and our life easier. We do so by going to restaurants that he prefers, taking trips that we know he'll do mostly well at, making these our regular experiences because they are familiar to him. But we also try to introduce Connor to new experiences. These outings come with stress because we are entering the unknown. Many times, he has surprised us by doing great at that outing and then we can add to our list of family activities. One of those that has changed over time has been flying. At first, he would have meltdowns during flights. We believe he didn't understand why we were sitting and had to be strapped in. Slowly but surely, he is doing better and better on each flight—maybe a meltdown here and there but nothing like when he was younger. Our boundaries are expanding.

When it comes to self-harm and harm to others, Connor's doing better as he gets older. We have the aid of a wonderful psychiatrist that has helped him with medications that reduce the severe meltdowns, those in which he self-harms. That gives us such great peace of mind because when he hurts himself, he can unintentionally hurt those around him as they try to calm him down. We are aware that he is now twelve years old, and hormones are raging—it's a phase we will have to endure and get past.

His autism is profound, which causes a lot of stress to our immediate family. He still wears a diaper at night, and we still have to watch him when he's doing No. 2 because he does not understand what it is to wipe. He doesn't get simple commands, such as "Get your shoes" or "Get your water bottle." It is very challenging but, every single day, I am committed to my promise: to love, to accept, and to understand.

Along with the key component of a parent's love, I also want to share some pointers with you that helped my family navigate this journey.

LEARN AND TEACH ABOUT AUTISM

Research, research, research. The more you know the better. You may feel overwhelmed at the start, but you will feel so much better when you sit in front of doctors, therapists, and specialists. When they use terms related to autism, you will know what they are talking about. With knowledge, you also can make more informed choices and advocate for your child with more confidence.

Many parents of kids with autism feel isolated, misunderstood, and unsupported. I felt that way so many times in this journey, too. At first, we found ourselves leaving gatherings early because we were so stressed dealing with Connor's behavior while family members told us, in the kindest of ways, how to handle a situation. It can be frustrating when your family doesn't understand your child's needs or your stress or when they question your parenting decisions. Because of this, gently teaching our family members about autism and sharing how we try to effectively manage behaviors has helped us so much in reducing family stress and improved the experience for all of us.

BUILD A STRONG SUPPORT NETWORK

Building my support network has been the best thing I have ever done because parenting a child with any type of special needs affects every part of your being. If you are anything like me, you will constantly worry about your child's autism and long-term well-being. So, it's great when you have someone to bounce thoughts off of and talk to. This can take different forms:

- For emotional support. Have a confidant, someone you know you can trust with your innermost feelings.

- For social support. Find a friend you enjoy spending time with—someone who takes you away for rest and relaxation or some fun times out on the town.
- For near-complete understanding and shared experience. Create a close-knit group of autism parents.
- I'm in a close group of five moms. We met in a social media support group and lived close to each other. We share dinners or lunches to talk about our lives, but we also have a lot of fun enjoying our time together. There is nothing better than when you are with people that totally get you.

STRENGTHEN YOUR RELATIONSHIP WITH YOUR PARTNER

At times, being married and giving of myself to my husband was difficult. In my mind, life was all about my children—and that can happen in typical parenting as well. It is important to work on your relationship with your partner so that you can be a better team. In our case, we try to have lunch dates or date nights to keep the relationship thriving. We do dinners and lunches at least four times a month. Yes! Hire a sitter for dinner dates and go out. On these dates, our rule is to have fun, no more than 5 percent "kids talk." The rest is supposed to be all adult conversation. It's incredible to see how connected I feel after one of those dates, especially when we stick to those guidelines. For a good laugh, I highly recommend comedy shows. We also go on couples' dates with non-autism parents. No autism talk there. It's so nice to have those breaks.

ACCEPT YOUR CHILD AND BE POSITIVE

Don't focus on your child's autism. Focus on their gifts. Appreciate those gifts. Celebrate even the smallest successes. Most importantly, stop comparing your child to others. Your child is unique.

It's impossible to predict our children's future. I know how easy it is to jump to conclusions! But, like everyone else, people with autism have an entire lifetime to grow and to develop their abilities. So don't ever, EVER lose hope.

This is something that life with Connor has taught me, and my promise of love strengthens me along the way. I am fortunate to feel this truly unconditional love for my son and his unconditional love right back. The way Connor's face lights up when he sees me walk into the room says it all. I wouldn't trade that amazing innocence he holds for the world. This little guy is truly the best.

I'd like to leave you with this, because this is what I have experienced in my journey thus far: We can handle much more than we think or feel. Every single difficult experience with our child builds our strength and ability to handle what comes next. You, too, can make that promise to love.

Resources
- *The Reason I Jump* by Naoki Higashida
- *In a Different Key* by John Donovan and Caren Zucker
- Anything by Mel Robbins—for personal development. After not working for some time, I felt scared, like I couldn't get back into a career. She has single-handedly pushed me just by listening to her advice.
- Documentaries: *Sounding the Alarm, A Mother's Courage, and Best Kept Secret.*

Podcasts:
- *Autism Live,*
- *Moms Talk Autism, and*
- *Uniquely Human*

Email: belqui@belquistwist.com
Website: www.belquistwist.com

Social Media
Facebook, Instagram, TikTok: belquistwist
LinkedIn: Belqui Ortiz-Millili
www.linkedin.com/company/belquistwist/

Hashtag
#AMothersPromise

My Love Letter to My Child

Connor,

You have brought so much joy to my life! I am so grateful that the one day you could have chosen to leave us, you didn't. You stayed. Ever since then and every single day, you have taught me so many lessons about how to be compassionate, patient, and loving. Nothing you can do will make me love you less.

You don't speak, and I know that you may never speak. But I will forever try to understand you when you express your sorrows or joys. I can see this joy but sometimes I wonder why you are so happy. I wish I could delve deep into your soul and learn all about you, even more than what I know now.

You have given me purpose. Being your mom is a gift. Every time you share your smile, I want to stop time and stay right there. Why? Because you are so pure. You have no malice, no grudges—you just love.

I promise, like I promised Natalie, that I will always be here for you. No matter what. Until the day that I am gone, you will be with me, and I will be your soft place to fall every single day.

Love,
Mami

BIOGRAPHY

Belqui Ortiz-Millili is an autism mom who is also a certified autism support coach, certified by The Institute for Professional Excellence in Coaching (IPEC). She has been recognized for her work by Neiman Marcus as one of their "Faces of Beauty" honoring women making a difference. Belqui has participated in many symposiums and parent panels on autism awareness and parent panels and resides in Arizona.

She spends most of her time as a chef, recipe developer, food blogger, and YouTuber. Belqui enjoys cooking for Tastemade and sharing her recipes on local television. Her concentration is Latin Caribbean Cuisine and Latin Fusion Recipes, and she has been featured in Panasonic and Walmart+ campaigns sharing her delicious Latin recipes. Of Dominican descent, Belqui credits her bilingualism to her childhood living between the Dominican Republic and the United States.

Before becoming an autism mom, Belqui was an actor in her hometown of New York City and appeared in *Law & Order and The Bill Cosby Show*. She also hosted *American Latino TV*. Belqui holds an advertising and marketing communications degree from The Fashion Institute of Technology in New York City. She is married to David Millili and has three children, Evan, Connor, and Natalie (RIP).

IT TAKES A SPECIAL MOM TO RAISE A SPECIAL CHILD

Letia Motley is the founder and owner of Be Yourself Hair Care, LLC. In her spare time, she volunteers by providing vital resources and information to parents/caregivers of children with different abilities. You can connect with her on Facebook, Instagram, or LinkedIn.

"His needs are constantly changing, so there will always be something for me to learn."

THE PREGNANCY

I thought telling my parents that I was pregnant at eighteen would be the most difficult part of being a teenage mom, but I was wrong. It was 2009, I was a senior in high school, and graduation was two months away when I found out I was pregnant.

Unfortunately, I was no stranger to being pregnant at such a young age. Six months prior I had been in the same situation and decided to terminate the pregnancy. Now, I was faced with another life-altering decision. Although this was my second time around, the emotional rollercoaster of making the "right" decision was worse. For the next two weeks, I mentally tortured myself about what I should do, but finally decided to keep my baby. Prom and graduation were right around the corner, so I decided not to tell anyone about my pregnancy until after those events. I went to prom and walked across the stage eight weeks pregnant without anyone ever knowing. Harboring this huge secret made it impossible for me to truly enjoy these moments.

About a month after graduation, my mom threw a trunk party for my sister and me. Friends and family came to celebrate us being college-bound and showered us with gifts that could fit in the trunk we would take with us. I still had not told anyone about my pregnancy, but I knew that I had to come clean after this party. To say that my mom was disappointed was an understatement. "Why, Letia?"

I remember her saying, "Why would you do this again? After we just went through the traumatizing experience of terminating your last pregnancy." The next few weeks were the worst. Friends and family were informed about my pregnancy, and then came the questions: "How did this happen?" "What are you going to do about college now?" I had no answers and, honestly, I just wanted everyone to leave me the hell alone.

Initially, I had planned to study audio engineering at Madison Media Institute in Madison, Wisconsin. But I didn't feel comfortable moving away from home while pregnant. So, a month before I was scheduled to start school, I had to come up with a backup plan. I stayed in Chicago and attended the Illinois Institute of Art. After completing my first semester, I decided to take some time off because my due date was approaching, and I knew that trying to juggle a newborn while attending college would be overwhelming. My pregnancy flew by. I didn't have any complications, morning sickness, or weird food cravings. After forty weeks of pregnancy, sixteen hours of labor, and four hours of pushing, I gave birth to a handsome baby boy on February 14, Valentine's Day, 2010. His name is Brent, and he is my lifelong valentine.

WHAT IS HAPPENING WITH MY CHILD?

The first year of Brent's life passed quickly and wasn't easy, but I had a lot of support from friends and family.

Brent was doing great; he was achieving all of his baby milestones. He was sitting up at three months, crawling at six months, walking at eleven months, and was able to say a few words by twelve months. However, around eighteen months I noticed that Brent had lost the few words that he was once able to say. He had completely reverted to babbling and baby talk and started to walk on his toes. Although I had never been around a baby prior to having Brent, I was sure that this new behavior wasn't "normal." I started to google these things in an attempt to determine what was going on with Brent and came across disorders that I had never even heard of before, such as autism, cerebral palsy, and muscular dystrophy. The next day I asked Brent's childcare provider if she had noticed anything different about him compared to other children his age. She gave me a warm smile and a phone number for early intervention. After four long days of in-home observations, early intervention determined that Brent would benefit from developmental therapy, occupational therapy, speech therapy, and physical therapy. Although I was happy that this team of therapists would be able to help, I still didn't have the answer to the million-dollar question: What is going on with my child? I asked Brent's developmental therapist, Megan Murphy, her opinion on what may have caused his word regression and toe walking; she didn't answer.

Still, Megan gave me what I later considered to

be some of the most important advice along our autism journey. She said, "Have Brent evaluated, and the doctor will provide you with an official diagnosis. You'll need this diagnosis to receive services for him in the future." I wasn't sure what she meant by "evaluated" or "diagnosis," but I contacted Brent's primary care pediatrician, who referred me to a developmental and behavioral pediatrician, Dr. Susan Fielkow.

Our first appointment with Dr. Fielkow was an intake appointment. Her first question was, "What brings you in today?" I shared my concerns and Brent's observation reports from his early intervention therapists. She listened to everything I had to say while taking notes at the same time and never once cut me off. Every few minutes she would observe Brent playing with the toys in her office, while still listening to me and taking notes. At the end of the appointment, she explained that she didn't like to prematurely diagnose children and felt that Brent was still too young for an official diagnosis. She recommended that we continue with the early intervention therapy and return in four months. I spent the next four months constantly observing Brent and trying to diagnose him via information on Google.

THE DIAGNOSIS: AUTISM SPECTRUM DISORDER

It was February 12, 2012, two days before Brent's second birthday, and we were at our second appointment with Dr. Fielkow. Prior to the appointment, the family and child advocate at Brent's childcare facility, Vivian Serwaa, had asked if she could accompany me to the appointment for moral support. It was like she already knew that I was going to receive bad news. Although I was nervous, I still felt a sense of joy because Brent was finally being evaluated. Soon, I would have an answer to my million-dollar question.

The evaluation process was much more exhausting and overwhelming than I could have ever imagined. In the first hour of evaluation, I answered questions about my pregnancy, delivery, family psychiatric and medical history, and I completed parent rating scale forms. I couldn't imagine applying some of these questions to Brent: "Does your child twirl, spin, or bang objects?" "Does your child have problems making eye contact?" "Is your child nonverbal?" "Does your child use an odd way of speaking?" It felt like I answered a thousand questions in that first hour and my head was spinning.

The doctor spent the next hour evaluating and observing Brent. She put Brent and me into two separate exam rooms, but I could see everything she was doing through a two-way glass. These weren't your typical doctor's office exam rooms. Brent's room was filled with toys, puzzles, swings, and trampolines, while mine looked more like a cozy family room. Brent's evaluation didn't seem as strenuous as mine. The doctor shared fun, age-appropriate activities with Brent and observed how he responded. She also asked a few age-appropriate questions, but at the time, Brent was considered nonverbal, so he was unable to answer.

At last, it was the final hour of the evaluation. The doctor reviewed the rating scale scores and observation findings: "Brent has autism spectrum disorder," she said. I looked at Vivian who said, "Are you okay?" I could tell from her expression that she was expecting me to break down and cry, but I didn't. I couldn't. I sighed with relief; I finally had the answer to my million-dollar question. As we were leaving the doctor's office, Vivian asked, "How are you feeling? Are you just in a state of shock right now?" I couldn't answer. I was feeling so many emotions that it was hard for me to put them into words. I wasn't shocked, though. Deep down in my heart, I had already known that it was Autism Spectrum Disorder (ASD). I knew from the very first time I googled his symptoms when he was eighteen months old. But like many special needs moms, I didn't want to admit it. I didn't want to admit that my son may not be "normal."

That night, I held Brent tighter and kissed his forehead again and again while I cried quietly.

I blamed myself for Brent's diagnosis. Did I not breastfeed long enough? Did I stand in front of the microwave while pregnant? Could there have been lead paint in my apartment building? I would always ask myself,

"Why is this happening to my son?" And for a long time, I only shared his diagnosis with my mother and his teachers. I was so worried about people judging us that I was too scared to share his diagnosis with anyone else. But then, my mom told me, "It takes a special mom to raise a special child." If I was going to be that special mom, I would have to learn as much as I could.

I became Brent's student, constantly observing and studying him. I learned his likes and dislikes. I learned what caused him to be overstimulated and how to best soothe him in those moments. I learned how to communicate with him while he was nonverbal. I learned the best methods for teaching him. I learned that he referred to people he loved as Dora because he loved Dora the Explorer. I read tons of books about autism and different forms of therapy. I watched YouTube videos. I attended autism seminars and expos. I networked with adults on the autism spectrum and other professionals in the field. I learned how to advocate for him. And I wasn't learning alone. After the diagnosis, I assembled a dream team to help me help him.

THE DREAM TEAM

Megan, Vivian, and Dr. Fielkow were godsends! Megan taught Brent and me how to communicate via American Sign Language (ASL) and picture exchange communication system (PECS). I learned that just because Brent was nonverbal, it didn't mean he didn't have anything to say. At two-and-a-half years old, he said his first word, "Please." I was so excited, I screamed! That moment gave me hope. I knew then that Brent would go on to accomplish great things, even if it took time.

Vivian coordinated partnerships with Brent's early intervention therapists and his childcare facility. This allowed his therapists the opportunity to work with him at home and at school. The therapists trained Brent's teachers on how to understand and communicate with him better. Vivian also gave me some of the most important advice as we transitioned from early intervention into the preschool special education system: "Know your rights. You and Brent have rights. Make sure you know them and are ready to advocate for your son."

Dr. Fielkow played a vital role in Brent's early detection and diagnosis. She provided me with all of the referrals, resources, and guidance needed to help Brent. She saw me as a valuable partner in his health and progress.

Kimberly Davis was Brent's third and fourth-grade teacher, and his private tutor for fifth grade. She's always had his best interest in mind, inside and outside of the classroom. We still talk to her—she's become a part of our extended family. She's resourceful and a dope person to know.

With the help of this team, I've watched Brent learn so much, even as I continue to learn from him.

OUR JOURNEY WITH AUTISM

Brent is now twelve and has been in a wide range of therapies since he was eighteen months old. He attends a full seven-hour school day, with anywhere from one to three hours of therapy immediately after, and he has never once complained. He's remained the same happy child through it all.

The hashtag #BeYourself is important in Brent's story because he has never been afraid or shy to be himself. He doesn't mask his autism to fit into what society has deemed to be "normal." All he knows is to be himself, to be Brent. Whether people like it or not he will always proudly be himself. He loves to sing and dance. He has made friends and built lasting relationships with some amazing people. He is the sweetest boy to everyone he meets. But most importantly, he is true to himself.

Brent recently graduated from Applied Behavior Analysis (ABA) therapy, and he's about to graduate from occupational therapy. On ABA graduation day he said, "I want to get cheesecake from the factory for my celebration," and we did just that. I have witnessed so many everyday miracles with him. He talks nonstop. He is happy, funny, and empathetic. Being Brent's student has taught me more than any book, class, specialist, or therapist ever could. He made me the special mom and woman that I am today. I know that he has a bright future ahead of him and will continue to achieve remarkable things. As Brent grows and makes progress, his needs change, so there will always be something for me to learn. I encourage all parents and caregivers who are constantly learning to enjoy the small wins and victories; that will provide fuel for big challenges.

Resources

- Kimberly Davis, MSW, learning and behavior specialist, Wilson dyslexia practitioner;
- davis.kimberlyv@gmail.com
- North Shore Pediatric Therapy, 4433 Touhy Ave., Unit 335, Lincolnwood, Illinois 60712 877-486-4140, www.nspt4kids.com

Email: gentletherapyslp@gmail.com
Website: www.beyoutuful.com

Social Media
Facebook: Letia Glanz
Instagram gentletherapyslp
LinkedIn: linkedin.com/in/letia-motley-06a093a7

Hashtag
#BeYourself

My Love Letter to My Son

Dear Brent,

You aren't like other children and that's okay! You have been a blessing in disguise. You have taught me to treasure things that most people take for granted. I have witnessed so many everyday miracles with you! Over time, I've become an advocate, educator, and specialist to the strongest little boy.

You have given me strength that I never even knew I had. You have changed me so much and I am nothing without you. You have shown and taught me the true meaning of unconditional love. You have taught me to listen to all the ways you are trying to communicate. You have taught me how to distinguish between what you choose not to do and what you aren't able to do. You have taught me that there is always a reason for the behavior and that reason has never once been just to annoy me. You have taught me about stimming and how it is sometimes necessary. You have taught me that fixations and echolalia serve a purpose. Being your student has taught me more than any book or therapist ever can. I've learned that the more I pay attention to how you think and respond, the better I understand you. Most importantly, you have taught me to stay true to who I am, always be myself, and to do what I want without fear.

I remember when you were first diagnosed. I reached out to a second doctor for a second opinion, and he told me about all the things you wouldn't be able to do. We never saw that doctor again and you have accomplished every single thing that he said you wouldn't be able to do. Never let someone tell you that you can't do something because YOU CAN! Never say that you can't because YOU CAN! Always remember to view your autism as a different ability rather than a disability.

You are my sunshine. I love you, always and forever.
Mom

BIOGRAPHY

Letia Motley is a strong, independent African American born and raised on the West Side of Chicago, Illinois. She has spent the last twelve years in the northern suburbs raising her children, Cree, Xavier, and Brent, and building her business, Be Yourself Hair Care, LLC.

She has received honorable recognition from several institutions: an advanced certificate in cosmetology from Harry S. Truman College, a pharmacy technician certificate from Chicago State University, and a bachelor of science degree from National Louis University. Letia was inducted into The National Society of Leadership and Success in 2019. Her long-term goal is to become a speech pathologist, and she is pursuing her Master of Science Degree in Speech Language Pathology with a concentration in applied behavioral analysis.

Letia dabbles in a variety of career choices and, most recently, served full-time as a supervisor at a home warranty company where she managed, traveled, and trained employees on claim authorization for homeowners nationwide. Soon, she will be taking her occupational therapy certification exam and her registered behavior technician exam. After passing these exams, she will serve as a certified occupational therapy assistant and a registered behavior technician.

Her experience with autism has given her the opportunity to meet amazing people. She enjoys networking with other members of the autism community. Letia volunteers by providing vital resources and information to parents and caregivers of children with different abilities.

In her spare time, she enjoys visiting with her granddaughter, Masterpeace, going on date nights with her husband, Christopher, and playing fetch with her dog, Charlie.

FULL OF GRACE

Alicia Gerez Graczyk is a justice of the New York State Court of Claims, sitting in the Supreme Court, Bronx County, Civil Term. She also serves on the board of directors of The Hagedorn Little Village School, Jack Joel Center for Special Children.

"Parenting a child with special needs is hard. The fear is real, but a lot of what we imagine is not."

As a justice, my craft is communication, but I find it difficult to put into words my own, personal experience with autism. There is so much to say as I have lived it, breathed it for so many years. Today, I celebrate my beautiful daughter, Grace, and the love, joy, and meaning her life has brought.

I was never one to dream about getting married and having children. My focus was always on education and my goal to become an attorney. I grew up in a tough environment, surrounded by drugs, poverty, and crime. I had blinders on and did not see or plan much past becoming a lawyer. When I was ready, I met a wonderful man who I married. I was full of hope and optimism for what life had in store.

And then sixteen years ago, my life took an unexpected turn after my daughter Grace was born. It was supposed to be the happiest time of our lives. Instead, we were forced to seek help as Grace presented serious, pervasive developmental delays within a few months of her birth. Grace did not respond to her name, make eye contact, smile, or mimic sounds or behaviors. She cried incessantly for hours on end without apparent reason. Grace did not crawl until the day after her first birthday and finally took her first steps at eighteen months old.

After failing to meet the traditional milestones, she was evaluated and began early intervention. Despite receiving a wide array of therapies for her global delays, Grace failed to progress. Ultimately, Grace was diagnosed at twenty-two months of age. Stunned, I sat and listened as I was told point-blank, "Your daughter has autism."

SQUARE ONE

The diagnosis devastated me. I was truly without any

power to change my circumstances for the first time in my adult life. I did not know how to help my daughter and I felt ill-equipped to raise her. In that moment, all my dreams and hopes for my daughter vanished. I was mourning the child that I thought I would have while coming to terms with the diagnosis. However, my love for Grace never changed or wavered. Instead, I felt more love and compassion than ever because I knew that she would face a lifetime of challenges.

All the while, I watched my closest friends have their perfect, "typical" children. I heard stories of the milestones their babies reached and felt I had nothing to contribute to these conversations. It became difficult to spend time with my friends because I would keenly feel my loss in having a child that was so different from the rest. While my friends were wonderful and sympathetic, it did not lessen the pain of watching their kids grow while my own baby lingered in some purgatory. I knew comparisons were unwise, but I could not help myself. I kept thinking, *why my child?* I was in so much pain that I could not see myself out of it. It took me a year to accept the diagnosis. It was hard, but prayer and therapy got me through.

Once I accepted it, I knew exactly what I had to do. As the mother of a special-needs child, I would have to become my child's advocate. My legal training was invaluable, though I would have to become proficient in the world of autism to fight for my daughter. As I immersed myself into this new venture, I researched all aspects of my daughter's treatment and her educational rights.

Although laws protect our children with special needs, many parents battle to obtain the services their children are clearly entitled to under the law. Navigating this labyrinth is difficult. Constant tension rises between counties denying services, and parents and providers advocating for children in need. Facing the county's limited budget and unlimited excuses is not for the faint of heart.

I advocated for Grace and obtained these services. However, Grace still failed to thrive. After early intervention ended at age three, Grace needed a specialized educational environment. She was not toilet trained, would not tolerate solid foods, and could not follow the simplest of instructions. Grace had pervasive deficits in speech and language and was unable to communicate, which brought constant tantrums. Without warning, she would drop to the floor and kick and scream for hours. We could not control her public outbursts and she self-harmed.

Then Grace was accepted to The Hagedorn Little Village School, Jack Joel Center for Special Children, the best specialized school in our region. Grace attended Little Village until age five and made great progress. She received classroom education as well as speech, physical and occupational therapies. I worked closely with the school during those years, and it was a productive collaboration. I attended conferences, workshops, and student events. Grace's teachers and therapists communicated with me weekly to ensure that I reinforced the skills they were teaching her at school in the home.

After Grace graduated from Little Village, I was invited to join the board of directors of the school, where I have served for the past eleven years. I accepted the position because it aligned with my desire to help autistic children and support their families. Little Village relies, in part, on private funding to provide innovative special education instruction to these children. As a trustee, I became an avid fundraiser for the school and raised assets that funded several new classrooms, which are now named after Grace. I also brought the knowledge I acquired parenting and advocating for Grace and used those experiences to help improve educational and support services for the children and families.

SHIFTING SYSTEMS, ALWAYS ADVOCATING

Just when I thought that I understood the system, Grace went to kindergarten at our local elementary school. She was in a self-contained class with other special-needs children. I was again back at square one because the school districts operate differently than early intervention. I started on my mission to learn New York education law to advocate for accommodations and services. Learning the system and making it work for Grace has been overwhelming and time-consuming. It is not a static situation. As Grace grows, her needs change, and school is an integral part of her growth.

At age six, Grace unexpectedly developed a seizure disorder. That was a particularly difficult time. I had learned how to handle the educational and social aspects of my daughter's autism, but now I had to consider her serious medical condition. Grace has had many seizures; at home, in school, and even at her birthday party. Most result in hospitalization. Grace takes anti-seizure medications daily, and we always carry an emergency medical kit just in case. The seizures are unpredictable; there are no warnings. It is traumatic to watch my girl experience these seizures and the after-effects for days later.

HER BEST LIFE

Nevertheless, despite numerous obstacles, Grace is living her best life! She is now sixteen years old and will be starting her junior year at our local high school. Due to the COVID-19 pandemic, and her underlying seizure disorder, Grace attended school fully remote for the end of eighth grade and freshman year of high school. She rose to the occasion and excelled at remote learning.

If anyone asked me years ago where I saw my daughter at this age, I would have said that I had no idea. If I was honest, I would have shared the picture that I had in my head for my daughter's future. I saw her attending a specialized school until age twenty-one and had no real hope for her future. Autism is not easy. It is not neat and tidy. Nuance fills the spectrum. I had no real expectation that she would lead a productive, happy, fulfilling life.

However, the reality is so very different from what I envisioned. My daughter is the happiest, most joyful person I know. She excels at science and math, currently taking chemistry and geometry. Grace is an accomplished surfer and surfs all summer long in our hometown of Long Beach, New York. She competes in our local Special Olympics every year and has earned several gold medals. She also has played on adaptive soccer and basketball teams. She has won several civic awards throughout the years. Grace is shy and reserved but comfortable around people she knows. She has a wicked sense of humor and knows a good joke when she hears it. Her sunny disposition endears her to those around her. She is sweet and kind; she is loved and respected. One of the greatest joys I experienced during her remote school days was listening to Grace argue with her teachers when she was told that she answered a test question wrong. She is an attorney in the making. Relentless. On several occasions, her teachers reversed her grades themselves because she makes compelling arguments.

Despite all of her greatness, Grace faces certain obstacles known to others on the spectrum. She is socially awkward and has difficulty making and maintaining friendships. She would rather spend her days on her computer or playing video games instead of engaging with others. While other children have suffered from the lack of socialization during the pandemic, Grace has thrived being home. It is sometimes an effort to get her out of the house if it is not to go surfing or swimming.

And yet, here is what I have learned so far: Parenting a child with special needs is hard. The fear is real, but a lot of what we imagine is not. I was always consumed with fear. I had so much fear that I missed so much. I could not enjoy many moments with my daughter because I worried about things outside of my control. Much of that worry was unwarranted. Grace is an amazing young lady and her father and I would not change a thing about her. She hopes and dreams. She wants to go to college, and I know she will. While in the past I dreaded her future, now I am excited for it. My advice to parents going through the same experience is to advocate for your child and never stop. But also, enjoy your children. Don't worry so much that you miss out on the greatness of your child.

While at times I still hurt for what wasn't, I no longer yearn for a different outcome. Grace is exactly the human being that God made her to be. She is uniquely herself and perfect in every way. She is loved beyond all measure, and her father and I could not be prouder. Our lovely daughter is so aptly named; she is full of Grace.

Welcome To Holland

by Emily Perl Kingsley

Copyright©1987 by Emily Perl Kingsley.

All rights reserved.

Reprinted by permission of the author.

I am often asked to describe the experience of raising a child with a disability—to try to help people who have not shared that unique experience to understand it, to imagine how it would feel. It's like this . . .

When you're going to have a baby, it's like planning a fabulous vacation trip—to Italy. You buy a bunch of guide books and make your wonderful plans. The Coliseum. The Michelangelo David. The gondolas in Venice. You may learn some handy phrases in Italian. It's all very exciting.

After months of eager anticipation, the day finally arrives. You pack your bags and off you go. Several hours later, the plane lands. The flight attendant comes in and says, "Welcome to Holland."

"Holland?!?" you say. "What do you mean Holland?? I signed up for Italy! I'm supposed to be in Italy. All my life I've dreamed of going to Italy."

But there's been a change in the flight plan. They've landed in Holland and there you must stay.

The important thing is that they haven't taken you to a horrible, disgusting, filthy place, full of pestilence, famine and disease. It's just a different place.

So, you must go out and buy new guide books. And you must learn a whole new language. And you will meet a whole new group of people you would never have met.

It's just a different place. It's slower-paced than Italy, less flashy than Italy. But after you've been there for a while and you catch your breath, you look around . . . and you begin to notice that Holland has windmills . . . and Holland has tulips. Holland even has Rembrandts.

But everyone you know is busy coming and going from Italy. . . and they're all bragging about what a wonderful time they had there. And for the rest of your life, you will say, "Yes, that's where I was supposed to go. That's what I had planned."

And the pain of that will never, ever, ever, ever go away . . . because the loss of that dream is a very, very significant loss.

But . . . if you spend your life mourning the fact that you didn't get to Italy, you may never be free to enjoy the very special, the very lovely things . . . about Holland.

Resource

- "Welcome to Holland," a poem by Emily Perl Kingsley.

Email: aliciamgerez@aol.com

Social Media
Facebook: Alicia Gerez Graczyk
Instagram: Aliciamgerez

Hashtags
#FullOfGrace #AmazingGrace #GodsGrace

My Love Letter to My Daughter, Grace

My Dearest Grace,

Happy Sweet Sixteen! It is amazing to see all you have accomplished!

When you were diagnosed with autism before your second birthday, your dad and I were so worried about your future. I wish I would have known then how wonderful you would turn out! Then I would not have worried so much.

You have known you have autism since you were nine. One day in the car, you asked "What is autism?" I was completely unprepared. "Where did you hear that word?" I asked. You kept repeating, "Autism Awareness." Back then, you spoke in phrases, not in full sentences. I looked back to where you were sitting. My car's Autism Awareness magnet was next to you on the back seat. After our last carwash, I had forgotten to put the magnet back on the bumper.

I knew we would have the "autism conversation;" I just didn't expect it so early. But you have always been so, so smart. I thought before I answered. This was a pivotal moment, our first conversation about autism. When I still couldn't come up with the right words, I said that autism meant that you thought and did things differently from other kids, but that you were as good, if not better, than those other kids.

Words failed me. Then and now, words still fail me.

I can't communicate to you just how wonderful you are. Though you were born with autism, it is not who you are, and it certainly does not define you. It is merely a condition with which you were born.

You, my dear beautiful girl, are the best human your dad and I know. We are madly, crazily in love with you and feel so lucky to be your parents. You are brave, and courageous, and you have the sweetest disposition, always happy, smiling and laughing.

You are kind to everyone you come across. You are a great friend, and you fiercely defend and stick up for your friends at school. We love that you still skip around everywhere, even though you're sixteen years old. You have the best sense of humor, and your dad and I love laughing with you.

You are intelligent and we recognize how hard you work. After you graduate, we are excited to see what the future holds for you. You will become what you set your mind to, and we will be with you every step of the way.

My sweet girl, you are the perfect daughter. You, dad, and I fit so well together. We are so blessed to be your parents. Always remember how much we love and cherish you.

Love,
Mom

BIOGRAPHY

Justice Alicia Gerez Graczyk was born in Brooklyn, New York. She became an attorney in 1996, and she more recently served as justice on the New York Supreme Court, Bronx County, Civil Division. She was appointed as a justice of the New York State Court of Claims in 2021. She married the love of her life, Phil Graczyk, in 2003, and together they have raised their beautiful daughter, Grace.

Gerez serves on the board of directors of the Hagedorn Little Village School, Jack Joel for Special Children, a school for children with special needs. Through word-of-mouth, her name has become synonymous with being an autism warrior. She has counseled parents on all aspects of autism, educational services, and the emotional toll of diagnoses. Prior to becoming a judge, she served as a parent advocate for parents with special-needs children and appeared before the schools' committee for special education, where services and accommodations are determined for these children.

In her personal life, Gerez loves the ocean and living in a beach town, where she watches her daughter surf every summer. She is a fitness enthusiast and enjoys traveling with her husband and adventurous daughter.

265

FOR THE LOVE OF A.J.

Adam Otero is a husband and proud father of two who has worked in finance for over twenty years. He loves to use his creativity and artistic ability to further autism awareness. He is also the creator of the Facebook page ASD Superhero League.

"My superhero is my son. He doesn't need a suit or a cape – he is his own symbol of hope."

I want to begin my story, or should I say our story, by stating that my amazing son is not autism. I have no desire for him to become the poster boy or symbol for Autism Spectrum Disorder (ASD). Please understand that I don't mean this with any negative undertone. I don't consider autism to be an evil affliction or a curse, but I refuse to let this one component of his life define my son. He is so much more than ASD. He's a jigsaw puzzle wiz, a crispy bacon connoisseur, and he has the most infectious giggle. That said, ASD is a big part of our daily lives and something that we face together as a family. As I contribute my perspective to raising a child with autism, I hope that I can make my son, A.J., proud.

GREAT EXPECTATIONS

Great Expectations is not just a title of some old book or movie, and I believe that every good, caring parent truly desires that their children surpass their own accomplishments and become better versions of themselves. Not in the way that "stage parents" want their kids to be famous so they can live vicariously through them, but for our kids to be bolder, braver, and wiser than we were and succeed where we might have fallen short. It could be an unfair aspiration, but we all do it. We want our children to take the chances we missed growing up, to avoid the same hardships we suffered, and to have every advantage life has to offer.

Before I had my son, I envisioned his extraordinary life. Everything from my son being a doctor to being the starting point guard for the New York Knicks—hell, why not both? Growing up on the Lower East Side of Manhattan, I was raised in an environment where most of us were unaware of ASD. I don't think I ever heard of autism until the movie Rain Man and, while that was a great film, it wasn't a true-to-life documentary. It couldn't highlight the complexity or the broad spectrum of ASD. The little I did learn from the film made me think that people with autism would not live full or enriching lives. They wouldn't have careers or a family and eventually would need to settle into assisted living because they couldn't live independently. It wasn't until later that I learned that there is an entire spectrum and that ASD doesn't prohibit a good life. Individuals with autism can lead a "full" life—it just requires more work and a different perspective to get there.

My wife, Sania, and I had gone through years of trying to have a second child. The news that we had finally gotten pregnant was one of the happiest days we shared as a couple. Later that year, on Christmas Eve, my wife announced we were having a boy to a room full of family and friends. I can't remember ever feeling more overwhelmed with joy, testosterone and, yes, a ton of those great expectations.

Right away, my mind started working to figure out which college he could attend (with the best division one basketball team), what kind of car he would drive, how many grandsons he would give me to carry on the family name. I imagined that I would teach him everything I ever learned and let him have a leg up on everyone else. Show him how to draw like a professional comic book artist, show him how to throw the perfect spiral football, and help him understand the difference between *Star Wars* and *Star Trek*. Teach him what kind of girls he should bring home to meet Mom. I planned every detail of his life five minutes after I knew I had a son. Everything was falling into place. I had married the love of my life and I was about to have a son. But as all of us know, life rarely goes according to plan.

We were living in Florida and a few weeks before my wife's due date, I was offered a job in the Tri-State area. Since Sania was in her third trimester and unable to travel, I had to go ahead alone and leave her, our teenage daughter, Serenity, and our yet-to-be-born son behind. Two days into working at the new job, my wife called me—she was going into labor. My brother, Milton, rushed me to the airport, so I could hop a flight and make it to the delivery room in time to see my son come into the world.

I was there to be the first person to see his perfect little face when he was born. All I could think about, holding this beautiful being ten minutes old, was all the amazing things he was going to be and how proud he would make us. We gave him my first name, Adam, thinking that if anyone could bring glory to that name it would be him. After a week, I returned to New York, leaving my family in Florida. When I was able to have them come and meet me in New York, I was so happy to have my family together.

As time went on, A.J. (Adam Jr.) developed "normally." Sitting up, babbling, crawling—all of the things you would expect from a baby. He started walking just before his first birthday and demonstrated fine motor skills and lots of eye contact. There was no indication, no red flags. He was enrolled in daycare at nine months and flourished. When A.J. reached age two, he still wasn't speaking, not even simple words like "no" or "mama." His pediatricians and other doctors assured us that there was nothing to be concerned about—the old bullshit that boys develop slower than girls. My family pointed out that I was an infamously late talker, not speaking until age four. Their assurance was enough for me to turn a blind eye. Still, my wife's intuition would not let her accept this, and at the first opportunity she had A.J. evaluated by another pediatrician, who initially diagnosed him with sensory issues. Sania worked on getting him support and early intervention with two great organizations, Sunny Days and Listening Partners in Orange County, New York. The therapists arrived twice a week and had him try to repeat simple sounds and play with uncooked rice. I was still in denial, believing it was nothing more than a need to adjust to different environments, sounds, and textures. After all, A.J. would engage with me, look into my eyes when I would tickle him, and in the measly two items I googled about autism, children with ASD couldn't do that. I didn't want to dig too deep. The thought of A.J. having something serious terrified me.

Things worsened when the daycare promoted A.J. to toddler class. Being nonverbal isolated him from the other children. Still, the instructor blamed A.J.'s "aggressive" behavior—that's what she called his screaming and throwing toys—as the reason no other kids wanted to play with him. Instead of recognizing it could be something more profound, the caretaker allowed my poor two-year-old son to play alone in the corner of a big room filled with other children. We soon started getting almost daily complaints about A.J. hitting a staff member or throwing a toy that hit another child. It was an ever-growing list of incidents until they called us both in to basically expel him from the daycare program. It was gut-wrenching. We trusted this daycare with our precious boy, and here they were telling us that they didn't want him there. Sania found another daycare that promised they were more than capable of handling A.J. and his sensory issues. They even flaunted a sensory room as a selling point. Six months later, they removed my son, claiming he was too much of a liability. My mother-in-law, Gloria, had to fly in from Puerto Rico to babysit him for the next few months. Over that summer, A.J. underwent multiple ear infections, and by year's end, we were encouraged to have him undergo surgery to place tubes in his ears. Again, doctors assured us that his lack of speech wasn't autism but hearing impairment or loss due to all the infections and that within two months after the surgery, we wouldn't be able to stop him from talking. The ear infections weren't as rampant after the surgery, but nothing changed with his behavior or speech.

We returned to his pediatrician seeking more answers. We were still told it wasn't anything of concern, but if we wanted to, we could see a pediatric neurologist. Sania made the appointment the minute she left the doctor's office. The next available date was three months away. We had plenty to keep us busy in those coming months, though: Serenity graduated high school, we relocated to a town closer to both of our jobs, and to top it off we went on a family cruise. A cruise vacation like that probably sounds like an amazing distraction. It was a nightmare. A.J. woke up every night at 3 a.m. and screamed so loud that passengers in neighboring cabins would bang on the wall. Coming home felt like a blessing until the day of the appointment with the neurologist. I couldn't go with my wife to the evaluation, but I remember the phone call. Sania calmly explained the diagnosis with a slight tremble in her voice that let me know she had been crying, "autism spectrum disorder." I told her it was OK in that non-emotional, macho way guys react to truly devastating news. I wanted to help soothe her pain as quickly as possible, so I wouldn't start sobbing. I choked back my tears and waited till she hung up so I could sit in my car, get all of my emotions out, and compose myself before I got home.

Receiving the diagnosis was a hard dose of reality I could have never prepared myself for. All those great expectations for my son's life faded. One of the hardest things about having your child diagnosed with ASD is that from the moment the doctor says, "Autism," you know that your child will endure an entirely different set of challenges. You may not know how to help them navigate and overcome them. I felt helpless.

A lot went through my mind when my wife relayed the diagnosis, but the most terrifying thought was, *Will I look at A.J. differently?* Now that we knew he was autistic and might not accomplish all the things I had dreamed, would it change the way I felt about him? I put on a brave face when I got home from work that day, and avoided looking my wife in the eye for fear of melting down, but my son, who couldn't possibly understand what was going on, knew I needed a hug. He held on to me tighter and longer than usual, as if to let me know without saying a word, "It's still me, daddy. Don't worry, I will be OK and will make you proud." The tears I tried to hold back rolled down my cheek. I was certain then that I could never feel any differently about A.J. He was not damaged goods or a hopeless cause, and I wouldn't let anyone else view him that way. From that day forward, I became more determined to help him become the man he is destined to be, instead of my own selfish vision of what I thought he should be. He is my son. That's more than I deserve, and all I could ever wish for.

THE LEARNING CURVE

My wife, true to form, was already figuring out what kind of therapy would help him and who we needed to contact to get A.J. the services he would need. I stood stunned, nodding in agreement but still in disbelief. The worst thing about denial is you can convince yourself that you're just being hopeful. This can become a bad thing when you rely entirely on a miracle to address something that only hard work, persistence, and intensive therapy can help. If you find yourself waiting for the day you wake up and your child no longer has ASD, then, like I was, you are fooling yourself. I wish I had taken the cue from Sania and been more proactive and advocated for services earlier. I regret not being more a part of that, and I praise, thank, and give Sania credit for all that she did.

From the day of the diagnosis, I set my mind to more than standing by and letting my wife figure it all out alone. I started reading anything I could find that would help my son. I researched the benefits of supplements, probiotics like Allstar Nutrition's Bio-Heal which improves gut health and helps minimize some ASD behaviors, and found an amazing agency, Applied ABC, that offered Applied Behavior Analysis (ABA) therapy, which the current special needs program he was in didn't provide. A.J. was blessed with some amazing therapists: Kelsey, Chelsea, Morgan, Noel, and Tashiana, who have all been instrumental in his progress. Sania was also able to get A.J. into a specialized school program, Abilities First, that works exclusively with children who have all forms of special needs. While we knew there was no quick-fix or miracle cure, we wanted to provide A.J. with anything that could help him achieve his full potential, whatever that might look like.

SILVER LININGS

A.J. started the Abilities First program the following fall. He began receiving ABA therapy after school and at home, and again all the pieces seemed to be falling into place for providing A.J. with support. Then the COVID-19 pandemic hit.

The initial wave of COVID-19 was the perfect storm of frustration, isolation, and fear.

My wife, who manages a medical practice, physically reported to her office every day, while I worked from home. Thankfully, the brokerage firm I work for knew I was caring for my autistic son, and they were *mostly* accommodating. Balancing an entire workday while caring for a child can be a daunting task for any parent, but if that child has ASD, it's damn near impossible to focus on anything other than your child's needs. A.J. is still not fully toilet-trained, which has caused issues in finding daycares and sitters as most require a child his age to use the bathroom on their own. A.J. is also mostly nonverbal, which causes him to engage in attention-seeking behaviors like screaming, climbing on furniture, or throwing objects. While everyone at work is sympathetic, they can't understand how my attention and time are stretched beyond limits in every direction. It's an overwhelming feat that I face daily.

While it's been brutal at times, COVID-19 did provide me with a rare opportunity to experience A.J.'s growth and development firsthand. I would have missed this if I was commuting to the office and my son was going to school and daycare. Weirdly, it has been a blessing as my bond with A.J. has grown stronger than I could have ever imagined. We're not only father and son; we are also best friends.

Even with the speech gap, A.J. and I communicate and connect in our own way. He now tells me, "I am hungry, eat" or even specific demands like "I want pancakes," "I want juice," or "please and thank you, Daddy," which he didn't do before ABA or the pandemic. One of my greatest fears was that he'd wander off, get lost, and not be able to tell anyone his name, his address, or even what town he lived in. Thankfully, he can now answer these questions. I can see him developing a sense of humor and trying to make me laugh with his little antics and funny faces. He doesn't just react to his environment. He has his own thoughts behind his actions. He has a definitive personality and can express himself. When my best grown-up friend, Joey, visits with his son, Jaxon, who's the same age as my son, A.J. is happy to see them and greets them with hugs and affection. When Serenity visits with her own daughter,

Kailani, A.J. gets so excited. He even allows Kailani to play with his toys, which he doesn't share with anyone else.

Don't get me wrong: he's come very far, but there's still a long way to go.

A.J. has yet to grasp the concept of danger, so he doesn't understand to look both ways when crossing a street, that he can't take toys or candy from strangers, and that you can't jump off everything that you can climb. I know that he will get there. That's not just blind faith, but my genuine belief that he will have a full and happy life with the proper support. Maybe he won't be a doctor or pro basketball player, but I never became the lawyer or second baseman for the Mets that my dad dreamed I would become. However, if my father were still alive, I hope he'd be proud of the man, husband, and father I did become as I will be proud of the man my son becomes one day no matter what he chooses to do with his life—as long as he lives it happily and without limitations. I still have great expectations for my son but they're more focused on the short-term. I don't care if he plays pro basketball twenty years from now, but I would love for him to be able to play a game of tag with his cousins.

I *hope* A.J. becomes a father. On that day when he realizes he's going to be a dad, what great expectations will he have? I know some might read this and think I'm delusional. That the *hope* my son will have a spouse and children is me slipping back into denial, but this is hope in its truest form. I'm not expecting him to be "cured" of ASD by divine intervention. I'm *hopeful* that the support we're providing him will allow him to have the best life possible. The line between denial and *hope* blurs, but when it comes to our children, we should always try to land on the side of hope. My favorite superhero used to be the one that wears the symbol of *hope* across his chest. Now my superhero is my son. He doesn't need a suit or a cape—he is his own symbol of *hope.*

Resources
- Sunny Days, Inc. for Early Intervention: www. sunnydays.com
- Abilities First: www.abilitiesfirstny.org
- Applied Behaviorial Counseling—Autism Therapy at Home: www.appliedabc.com

Social Media
Facebook: ASD Superhero League
Instagram: asd_superhero_league

Hashtags
#Destined4Greatness #MySuperhero

My Love Letter to My Son

To My Superhero,

A.J., you are my superhero. You may not come from a distant galaxy with a red sun, but you see the world in a way that no one else does, which makes me want to see the world through your eyes. You make me want to be a better man and an even better father.

You teach me patience.
You teach me humility.
You teach me as much as I could ever teach you.

You show me unconditional love.
You show me determination.
You show me my strengths and my weaknesses as you are my sun and my kryptonite.

You give me purpose.
You give me resolve.

You give me pride. I don't know if you will ever read this and feel the love that I have for you. You are not just a part of me, you are the very best parts of me. You are my greatest creation. You are my masterpiece. All that is good, right, and pure in this world can be heard in your laughter and seen in your smile. I want nothing more than to take this whole world and mold it into one that makes sense to you.

You, unfortunately, have my ears and my bad temper.
You, thankfully, have your mother's perfect nose and
empathy, your sister's pretty eyes and affectionate nature.
You have all of our hearts.

You make me proud.
You make me brave.
You make me immortal . . . with you as my legacy, I will live
beyond my time here on earth.

I love your hugs.
I love that you are ticklish.
I love the way you say our name: "Adam."

I love your autism because without it, you wouldn't be
you. It means you will never be mediocre. You will always
be extraordinary. It means every stride you make is a tiny
miracle. You perform miracles every day. You beat the odds
every day. You are a fighter like your mom, and, like your
mom, I have loved you since I first laid my eyes on you. I
will love you eternally and infinitely.

I will always be your protector, even when you grow
taller than me.

I will always willingly sacrifice my body and soul to
spare you harm or pain.

I will love you beyond time and space, to the moon
and back.

I pray that you will one day have the opportunity to
have a son or daughter that you love as truly and as deeply

as I love you. Only then could you possibly comprehend this feeling of true joy and accomplishment that you have given me.

You make my life complete—so much like the old symbol for autism, you have been the blue, curvy-edged, missing puzzle piece that I have searched for my whole life.

I love you, my son, my legacy, my Superhero.

BIOGRAPHY

Adam Otero was born and raised in the lower east side of Manhattan. In his childhood, his family struggled with poverty and lived in the housing projects where life for a young male Latino was tough. In the 1980s, options seemed limited. If you weren't in a gang, a drug dealer, or common thug, you were easy prey to those who were. The one advantage Adam had was that both of his parents were hardworking, strict, and, most importantly, present. Their guidance and vigilance provided him with a strong work ethic and a moral compass that helped him avoid many pitfalls. After graduating from Murry Bergtraum High School early at sixteen, he followed the footsteps of his older siblings with a career in finance while casually pursuing his passion in art.

Today, Adam has over twenty-five years of experience in finance, clearing, and brokerage back-office operations. He attended undergraduate courses at the School of Visual Arts in Midtown Manhattan. In his spare time, he is an anime, cartoon, comic, and graphic artist whose images and illustrations have been used primarily by independently published authors. He has provided original artwork for small businesses, corporate events, and individuals for logos, advertising campaigns, and other promotional purposes. Adam's aspirations include developing a series of children's books that are not just inclusive but focus on characters that represent many areas of the special needs spectrum. Adam directs his focus on his family and in helping his son achieve greatness.

BEHIND THE CAMERA: LIFE AS AN AUTISTIC PHOTOGRAPHER

———

Mike Catuara is a photographer for *Glancer Magazine* and Lifetouch.

"Don't judge me for what I am; judge me for who I am."

In 1970, when I was three years old, my parents were informed that I had autism, but didn't tell me. When I was twelve, my mother said that my behavior was caused by a chemical imbalance of the brain, but it wasn't until I was nineteen when the word "autism" was introduced to me. I remember looking it up in the World Book Encyclopedia because I didn't understand what it was at first, but as soon as I did, I understood. However, even though my parents didn't tell me I had autism, they did the best that they could to make me who I am today.

My relationship with my family was like any other family; I had my mother, father, and younger brother. I have always been closer to my mom than my dad but that doesn't mean I wasn't close with him. Mom was like any other mom, loving and supportive, and I thank her for moving me through those trials and tribulations that she went through raising me. It wasn't easy, but she made it work. My brother was also there when I needed him. Our natural sibling rivalry was common—like the saying goes, "They're not always friends, but they're always family." That describes us. As good of a relationship as we have, he has let me fight my own battles, which has taught me how to stand up for myself. This, I'm grateful for. One thing I know for sure is that no matter what, my family will always be there for me. I don't have to worry about who will take care of me because I know someone, whether my mom or my brother, always will. When I told my parents that I wanted to be a photographer, they were proud of me, which showed that no matter what I chose to do, they were going to be cheering me on every step of the way.

Before I found out I was autistic, I knew I was different from others. One of the first moments I noticed was when I was in kindergarten. Normally, children this age would get in trouble, but I never knew what was going on when I did, which led to doctors realizing I had some sort of problem. From then on, I was seen by psychiatrists, psychotherapists, and many other types of therapists. It would have been nice to know that I was autistic when I was younger because if I knew I was different than everyone else, I could have found a way to adapt much earlier on. Here's the thing: you will not be able to understand me until you see the world from my point of view. If I had any regrets back then, I would have done something to change the outcome.

Amazingly enough, some people who are autistic obtain special skills that are considered beyond levels of genius. Savants, such as myself, show skills, such as mathematical, artistic, musical, spatial, and mechanical abilities. I discovered I had perfect pitch when I was around eleven, yet never stuck to music. I could remember a long list of certain things, yet I couldn't remember other life essentials. Autism gave me the skill to compose photos the right way using the "rule of thirds" method of composition and design graphic trademarks and logos quickly, which was what I originally wanted my career to be based on.

I faced many obstacles, especially before reaching my career now as a photographer. Throughout my life, I have had people judge my capabilities because of my autism, and every time they did, I would show them otherwise. They assume that because I have autism, I can't do the things that people normally do. When I decided that I wanted to drive, there were some doubts because of the responsibilities of handling a vehicle, but I practiced anyway. I remember failing my first driving test and knowing that I wasn't going to let it end this way. I wanted to prove to myself that this was something that I could do and will do. Even when I thought I was a pro at driving, I still got tickets and got into a couple of accidents, but that doesn't mean I gave up. People make mistakes, get back up, and continue on. That being said, I couldn't just pick up a camera and make a career out of it. I had to gain experience and form a portfolio, which I didn't know how to do at first, but I knew that I had to start somewhere.

I remember the first time I became interested in photography. I had seen some of my friends' photo albums with a bunch of pictures that they took during the times that they had fun. And I figured, *well, maybe I can do something like that.* It wasn't until my upper-class years in high school that I thought that going to events, such as school dances and pep rallies, and capturing those moments in photos could be a lot of fun. I purchased my first camera with my own money that I had saved up. Though it was a used model, it still did the trick. I started to take pictures of every moment that I wanted to document and that was where my love of photography started growing. It's like photography was in my blood because I knew from the start how to position the camera and get perfect angles.

When I first thought about going to college, I thought, "What's a guy like me doing here?" My doubts were fighting with my aspirations, but I knew I wanted to be like everyone else. I wanted to achieve great things and showcase my work. But could I pull it off? I decided to try and applied to a community college. After a year of taking classes that were relatively easy, I was ready for a bigger challenge and enrolled at Illinois State University to pursue a bachelor's degree in graphic design. As much as I loved photography, I didn't know that I could make a career out of it, so I decided to pursue the other thing I loved and could actually have a degree in.

University was much harder than community college. The general classes that I had to take in order to graduate had nothing to do with my degree, which was frustrating because I was hyper-focused on only taking the classes necessary for graphic design. Because of this, I found it hard to excel in the general classes and ended up failing some of them, but that doesn't mean that I was ready to let these classes get the best of me. I did what I needed to do and found the resources necessary for me to push through those classes and excel. Still, I took photography classes during university because I wanted to keep this gift that I had alive. With those newfound skills, I started doing photo albums to keep those memories for a lifetime and eventually ended up as a freelance photographer for the school yearbook. The resources that were available to me while I was in college were the reason that I was able to graduate within four years. This was the best turning point of my entire life. Without those resources, it would have been tough for me to continue because the classes weren't adapted to my way of learning. Despite everything that I had been through because I am autistic and learn differently, I was now able to call myself a college graduate and, even better, a college graduate with a degree in something I loved to do. It wasn't easy, but I just couldn't give up.

Many autistic individuals don't have the capacity to keep up with a full-time or part-time job, unless, of course, it relates to their specialty in their God-given talents, such as art, music, photography, etc. They may lack certain skills from the corporate perspective. Throughout college, I had taken small jobs, at Taco Bell and Builder Square, to get me through paying for school but that wasn't what I wanted to do for the long run. I knew that I was capable of getting a better job and proving that the skills I had were useful to the world. The only thing I gained from those small jobs was the ability to buy better cameras to make my photos a better quality. When I graduated, I thought I would just simply jump up into the corporate ladder and contribute my skills as a graphic designer right away. But then the recession hit and, the next thing I knew, I couldn't seem to get myself a decent job until 1995. When I was finally able to get a job, it wasn't like I was handed one right out of college. It took time for a company to accept me. I started working for a company as a graphic designer, but after twenty-two years there, I needed something where I could shine even more and be valued. Slowly, I began realizing that I wanted to pursue photography as a career and, after sending my portfolio and letting my pictures do the talking, I landed the job as an events photographer with *Glancer Magazine.*

After eight years of struggling as a graphic designer, I decided to quit that field and do photography full-time. Finding other photography jobs wasn't easy, but I knew that I wanted to keep doing this, so I kept looking. In 2019, after applying many times, I got an interview with Lifetouch and once again, I let my pictures do the talking, which landed me the job. Working as a photographer for Lifetouch and *Glancer Magazine,* I can now make myself be seen and heard in doing what I love. I enjoy contributing to the Illinois High School Association (IHSA) as a senior school sports and events photographer and, at the same time, being a lifestyle photographer at social events in Chicago's western suburbs.

While working with Glancer, I have had the opportunity to take beautiful pictures of events and meet many amazing people, one being Tamika. We met through The Autism Hero Project (AHP), which promotes autism acceptance and changes the way the world views autistic individuals by also promoting inclusion in the business world. Tamika was in search of autistic professionals to contract at The Autism Hero Project Gala and, upon seeking help from a Facebook group, she connected with me. During the gala, Tamika highlighted the abilities of autistics and promoted businesses to participate in inclusive practices and challenged them to hire autistics in their own organizations. She spoke about how AHP was making a difference and the importance of raising awareness and acceptance for the autistic community. She then spotlighted all of the autistic people that were working the event from the young autistic teenager that they commissioned to make all of the art awards, to the videographer and me as the photographer. I was so inspired by the event that I felt the need to take the microphone and speak to the attendees and express how I felt privileged and honored to become an ambassador for autism. I want to let people know that there is hope.

As a photographer, I have no personal favorite person, place, or thing. I always have an eye for capturing attractive people, but primarily it's certain types of high-end social events (fashion shows, dances, parties) as well as low-light sunsets, evening skies, night cityscapes and neon signs, especially in Las Vegas. I had a great time during my senior year in high school, and believe it or not, was obsessed with Vegas lights as early as age six. Perhaps everything that reminds me of Vegas and past high school upper-class events inspires me to choose my best pictures. We live in an age where everything has gone digital. Film is now history, and digital photography now allows me to practice more than ever before by seeing instantly what I take and edit on a computer without the cost of expensive film and processing. I don't know where I would be without it.

My life doesn't end with achieving my dream career. I have other dreams for myself, too, like owning a house, traveling more, meeting new people, breaking boundaries, and getting out of my comfort zone to show that I can and will achieve anything with the right mindset. I also hope to someday naturally find someone that is right for me, maybe as I travel, but why should I worry about dating right now when I'm trying to do things to lead me to the path of independence? If I find someone, they need to be supportive and love me for who I am. As for getting married, that is something I might have to think about still, even at the age of 54 because, in Vegas language, it's either a seven or a crap!

I have never let my autism get in the way of how I want to live my life. Sure, it has formed some obstacles, but knowing how to jump over them and get to the finish line is what life should be about. I encourage parents to teach their children that although they can't change their diagnosis, they can change what people think they are capable of doing and show that having autism isn't something that they should be ashamed of. Being a person with autism is not any different than any other person. You should live the best life that you can. It's all up to you now as parents to give, speak out, and fight for more to be done for research, care, therapy, and hope. I only wish we could have done so way earlier when I was diagnosed. Then again, with help from my family and friends, my journey with autism made me who I am. I think that now is the time to make a difference in my life and other people's lives.

I cannot take the past fifty-plus years of my life and condense them down into a short interview that explains my complete journey, nor do I want to give parents of autistic kids who are reading this false hope over their future. But all I can say is that it's time to do something about autism. For people with autism, this is the advice I have for you: Be yourself. If you want to get the job, tell them what you do best and go with the flow. If you have a job that you love and an opportunity, don't over-exaggerate yourself and instead let your work do the speaking. Focus on your specialty and what you like to do best and never give up practicing so that when the time comes, you have something great to show them. I'm doing things that many never had the opportunity for, autistic or not. I'm living a good life and I thank autism for helping me embrace it. Don't judge me for what I am; judge me for who I am.

Resources

- Autism Speaks: www.autismspeaks.org
- The Autism Hero Project (AHP): www. autismheroproject.org
- Turning Pointe Autism Foundation: www. turningpointeautismfoundation.org
- Little Friends, Inc.: www.littlefriendsinc.org

Email: mcatuara@gmail.com

Website: www.mcatuara.wixsite.com/mcphoto

Socialmedia

Facebook: Mike Catuara Photography

Instagram: mcatuara3

Hashtags

#BehindTheCamera #LetYourWorkSpeak

My Love Letter to Autism

Dear Autism,

If it weren't for you, I would not have been me. I would have not had the best understanding of myself. You gave me the power to have better clarity of who I am in my world and the world in general. You gave me the power to excel in my chosen area and gave me the opportunity to push on and find who I am. You helped me break the boundaries of normalcy and helped me fit in despite my differences.

I am different, but that's OK. Nobody is perfect.

You gave the people around me the knowledge to understand and accept people like us. You gave me the ability to be able to learn the things that I am supposed to learn later on in life, like drive a car, handle my finances, and obtain a job—things that I feel are what I needed to create a happy and sufficient lifestyle for myself. Of course, I still have my faults and my hang-ups, but they are nothing in comparison to what I focus on and that is the man I chose to become. Thank you, Autism.

Sincerely,
Mike Catuara, an autistic photographer

BIOGRAPHY

Mike Catuara is a photographer and graphic artist in the Chicagoland area. He works for *Glancer Magazine* and Lifetouch, scouting senior school sports, capturing social events, and framing lifestyle photography throughout Chicago's western suburbs.

Mike has a bachelor's degree in graphic design from Illinois State University, and before photography, he worked as a graphic artist. His interest in photography stemmed from high school, where he found his knack for photography.

Mike enjoys capturing photos from social events to portraits to landscapes, but some of his favorites include sunsets. He continues to expand his skills, advocating for himself and other autistic people who wish to live fulfilling lives and exercise their gifts. To see Mike's work, visit his portfolio site.

SPECIAL PLANS

———

Ana Carolina Uribe Ruiz is a mentor for aviation and STREAM (science, technology, robotics, engineering, arts, and math), an international private banking and insurance professional, a special education advocate, author, and pilot. Connect with her on Instagram and LinkedIn.

"For I know the plans I have for you," declares the Lord, "Plans to prosper you and not to harm you, plans to give you a hope and a future."
–Jeremiah 29:11.

WHEN GOD HAS A DIFFERENT PLAN

Motherhood is simply amazing. Everything must be in tune for pregnancy and then to bring a life into this world—isn't that extraordinary? My grandmother used to remind me that it is not just the bringing of life into the world itself that is key; it's what we do next that is the most important. And that is true. Many mothers bring children into their lives not only by birthing them, but by loving them as their own.

When my son, Jose Maria, was born, he was given an incredible amount of love not only from us as parents but also our immediate family. I was a late mother, so he was a gift. Then the mental "bucket list" I had created for him started: first steps, first words, music class, playtime, art class, pre-kindergarten, elementary school, middle school, high school, university . . . In the process of checking those off came the challenge. This challenge strengthened our faith, made us look for solutions, consult with experts, and it still leads us to work together every day to do what is best for our child and for our family. The bucket list had to go.

When my son was eleven months old, he had a cold and could not sleep. My mother's intuition kicked in. Something was not the same, something felt different, something was out of place. I took Jose Maria to the doctor and went home, but a voice was still telling me something was wrong. I followed my instincts, called the ambulance, and took him to the emergency room. He had pneumonia. We transferred him to a different hospital into the intensive pediatric unit. If I had not followed my instincts, he would have been intubated. Who knows what the outcome could have been? But as the granddaughter of a pediatrician and a daughter of an amazing mom who told me to follow my gut, I listened to my intuition. Jose Maria stayed in the hospital for a week until everything was better. It was his first Christmas, and we spent it in the pediatric ICU.

Motherhood comes with an internal wisdom, an internal voice, intuition. When you have a child, it becomes second nature. Listen to that voice, even if it means you have to embrace the unknown or make sacrifices.

YOU HAVE A SPECIAL-NEEDS CHILD

At two years old, Jose Maria stopped responding to his name. At times, it seemed that he wouldn't respond depending on the question. He didn't pay attention the same way. Again, something was not right. After a conversation with another mother, I took Jose Maria in for an observation. I expected maybe one or two specialists would talk with us and offer some advice. But when we walked in, we were met by a psychiatrist, a psychologist, an occupational therapist, a speech and language therapist, a Board-Certified Behavior Analyst (BCBA), a special education teacher, and an assistant. I instantly felt small, outnumbered, and out of place. While I observed through one-way glass, the specialists spent three hours with my son. Then I received a yellow paper with an initial diagnosis: "your son has Pervasive Developmental

Disorder-Not Otherwise Specified (PDD-NOS)." Then they told me that my next appointment should be with a neurodevelopmental pediatrician. That was the kicker. I left mad as hell, stormed into the pediatrician's office, and grabbed his shirt, saying, "You should have told me!" After he calmed me down, he explained the autism spectrum. The spectrum held more complexity than I could understand at the time—how could Jose Maria have autism? He was a social child.

My world turned upside down. The next day, I received a call from the school district, "I will be your case manager. Come tomorrow with your husband and we will draft a plan for your son." A case manager? A plan? What is happening?

At the meeting, our case manager, a calm and collected psychologist, sat us down and explained what the state does, what resources were available, what the future steps were: therapies, occupational and speech, and starting school. At the time, Jose Maria was only two-and-a half years old. He was going to start preschool at three. When he started school, he was as happy as you can imagine. Seven kids, five adults, for four hours a day. Meanwhile, I cried for three weeks when I left my son at school, and the principal used to receive me with a box of tissues after I dropped my son off in class.

Through it all, my husband, Daniel, was a rock. Though he was ready to be with me in tackling what was coming, he also gave me the space to react to the emotions from receiving Jose Maria's diagnosis. I did the same for him when he needed space and time.

Daniel often helped calm my son, talking to him slowly, sitting on the floor with him. We learned to all play together. Daniel takes Jose Maria's hand and walks with him. I am truly blessed to have a husband and a father that is and always has been involved with our son. This support, this love, through a difficult time is something that carried me through, especially then, but also now, with every challenge we encounter.

DAILY CHALLENGES

Were there challenges? Too many to count. For example, tantrums at the supermarket—he had the lungs for that. I would pick up my screaming child, leave all the groceries in the cart, and head to the parking lot to drive home while everyone looked at me like a bad mother who couldn't control my kid.

When you take your child shopping or on a walk and people see him doing something different, someone may ask you if something is wrong. I always turn those moments into a teaching moment! "He is autistic," I tell them. "He may do some things differently, but he's good, thank you for asking." I suggest you take this opportunity, too. Maybe introduce your child in these circumstances because sometimes you can make a new friend and sometimes it really is a great teaching moment.

Some days are better than others. Our kids need attention, unconditional love, always a smile, but they really hate it when you say, "No." How do you handle their reaction to that no? You can explain the reason for no to a typical child. But for autistic children, well, the explanation needs to be done differently. Sometimes, you have to show them the reason you are telling them no. That can prove difficult, right? It's a longer process. With time, they will get it. That is the hope.

For example, Jose Maria did not like to talk much. He had the vocabulary, but his responses were short and concise. Why bother to say a full sentence if you can get something with one word? I learned to adjust so he used words he knew. When he asked for something as simple as water—one word, easy to understand, I used to sit and wait. He would struggle for a second, look at me like a mad guy, and then say, "Can I have water?" Priceless!

SOCIAL INCLUSION

One of the most difficult things to navigate when having a special kid like mine is other people and friends. Part of the issue is the people around you. While a few friends will come to you and give you a hug, ask you how your child is doing, how school is, or offer to have a coffee, many may not know what's happening or how to react.

Now, my son is a teenager, and he has different interests and needs: music, friends, outings, parties. He has never been invited to neurotypical party. He does not know what that is. Instead, we would invite "regular kids" (neurotypical ones) to our house. We have been blessed that Jose Maria has a few friends who understand his difference but challenge him. These friends focus on strong conversation, redirect Jose Maria so he is present, paying attention, understanding what he understands, and sharing what he wants to share.

These friendships developed when Jose Maria was in second grade. I met with a few moms and explained who my son is, how he was different, how he loves to be around people. That allowed friendships to flourish and continue! Yes, he loves his friends and chats today with all of them via Zoom, WhatsApp, or text, and those friendships have stayed strong. It is nice to see these kids, who are already seniors in university, stopping by to see him.

ADULTHOOD AND ADVOCACY

Jose Maria is nearly an adult, and we know that different challenges await us. He is becoming more independent. He can stay home alone for a short period, understand that we are going to do something, follow us along the way. He can always talk to us on FaceTime when he needs to do something before we get home. These are small steps but strong steps of growth and independence.

The most difficult part for us is that my son is social. This is a trait that many autistic kids don't have. They lack that social piece. My son is just the opposite but that also has a huge challenge. He might invite anyone home to see his collections or opens the door to strangers. He thinks it's okay to talk to everyone. That has been a long, difficult teaching experience. Now he understands better that when he is home alone, no matter who knocks on the door, he should not answer. And if something is unusual in his mind, he will call us or text us. We are always in constant communication.

At the same time, my husband and I have focused on remembering each other, our marriage, and the love we have, even as we guide Jose Maria. So, Daniel and I found common ground: we are both pilots and we love to fly together. Our freedom is in the air. Now that we have some time to get away, our dates are a light lunch or breakfast, half a day, here or there. It is not easy to find the right person to stay with our son—and we continue to adjust.

Jose Maria proves to me that just because he is almost an adult does not mean he is done learning. The educational system thinks that when they get to eighteen nothing else needs to be taught. They are wrong!!! What a challenge it is to fight with a system that thinks because they are legal adults, our children should not continue to learn important skills. It is here that you need to challenge the system the most. These young adults still have so much to learn, explore, and practice. The educational system keeps them until they turn twenty-two, with transition programs that are supposed to help them learn a trade and prepare them for the world. But that rarely happens. They teach some basic skills, like making change at a store, but we need more. Every child is different and has different needs and these needs should be customized and differentiated on their specific abilities and needs. We need to be able to have both open communication with the school district and still give push back when they are not meeting your child's needs.

Another issue is helping your child find employment. Companies who could employ these kids will give excuses. Under the law, businesses should have adults with disabilities as part of their workforce. Some businesses will tell you that they have a program, and when you try to see what it is, they give you the run-around. Or they will tell you, "We're trying to get a program," or "We had that, but it is not open…" It is here that every parent needs to advocate and challenge the system. Our children have a right to become more independent, they have a right to learn a new trade, they have a right to work. But they can't get there alone and need to be met where they are at.

Remember that bucket list? That went out the window way back then. Plans needed to be drafted based on our son, his time, his needs. Now, the next thing for Jose Maria is to find employment. He is currently getting training in retail and talking to several companies. For all of us, it's one step at a time, celebrating the victories, working to make and carry out new plans, and praying. I remind myself of God's word, "For I know the plans I have for you. Plans to prosper you and not to harm you, plans to give you a hope and a future." (Jeremiah 29:11).

Resources
In New Jersey:
- The Department of Education/Project Child will test children to see if they are under the umbrella of special education. After testing, they'll assign you a special education case manager, schedule a follow up with a neuro-developmental pediatrician, and send you local resources: www.nj.gov/education/specialed/childfind
- The Eden Institute: edenautism.org
- In California:
- Parents Helping Parents is one of the largest local resources for families and has been open for more than 40 years: www.php.com
- The Golden Gate Regional Center: www.ggrc.org

Social Media
Instagram: acuriberuiz
LinkedIn: www.LinkedIn.com/in/anauriberuiz
Twitter: uribe_anac

Hashtag
#SpecialPlans

My Love Letter to My Best Friends

To My Best Friends,

Love is a feeling, a sentiment, a time, a passion, a touch, an embrace. Every time I see my husband, Daniel, and my son, Jose Maria, my life is full.

Daniel, thank you for being my best friend, my partner, my lover,

The hand that gives me comfort,

The heart that keeps my love,

The patience when I am in the middle of a storm.

You allow me to be me every time I decide I need to embark on something new.

My passion to have our kid, and many like him, be heard, to have a voice, to have a choice,

For having my back when I am down

Or to celebrate the small things together with our son

And for just loving me just the way I am

Thank you for our son, for our love of flying, and for the time we are together.

I am so proud of you and my son.

Jose Maria, you are a special kid, and we see you with love, with understanding. You have taught us the amazing wisdom in listening, you have taught us to guide you, how to be ourselves around you, how to love you more than life. This is a gift.

I am absolutely blessed to have you in my life.

I love you!

BIOGRAPHY

Ana Carolina Uribe Ruiz was born and raised in Ecuador, attended law school, and came to the United States to study finance in Florida. She became a local banker and then an international private banker. She met her husband and moved to New Jersey. Her son, Jose Maria, was born in 2001.

When her son was diagnosed, Ana became a fierce advocate for her son and the autism community. She believes that we must make a difference for these kids and young adults. Her current focus is on creating opportunities for people on the spectrum to find meaningful employment and secure steps to independence.

In addition, Ana is a mentor for science, technology, robotics, engineering, arts, and math (STREAM), showing young girls that they belong in these fields.

Ana also has a great love of flying, which she shares with her husband. As a private pilot, she advocates for women in aviation, and received the Jefferson Award for Public Service in 2014 for her advocacy, having organized introductory flights for more than 400 girls and women in the Bay Area of San Francisco. She is co-president of the San Francisco Bay Area Women in Aviation International (WAI) Chapter and the founder of the WAI Costa Rica Chapter. She also is a Ninety-Nines International Organization of Women Pilots council member and a contributor to the book, *Latinas in Aviation*.

ASPIRITECH: AN INTERVIEW WITH CO-FOUNDER BRENDA WEITZBERG

Aspiritech is a world-class quality assurance (QA) testing company that empowers individuals on the autism spectrum to fulfill their potential through meaningful employment combined with social opportunity. From a kitchen table start-up, Aspiritech now has over 120 employees in two locations and continues to grow.

"We need a spectrum of opportunities for those on the spectrum."

Tamika Lecheé Morales: Tell us a little bit about your autism story and what it was like back then with resources and the lack of awareness when you got your diagnosis.

Brenda Weitzberg: *Raising our son, Oran, who was born in 1979, had its challenges. From age three to eight, we received multiple diagnoses including insufficient parental limits and sensory integration disorder. At eight, he was diagnosed with PDD-NOS and only at age fourteen (in 1993) did we first hear the term Asperger's syndrome. We couldn't find any technology and there were very few resources at that time that could help him or us.*

Oran, who permits us to share his story, had many areas of strength. He had taught himself to read in two languages at age three and had an extensive vocabulary, but he also had complex challenges, especially in the social, motor, and executive functioning arenas. These impacted his ability to be organized and planful, manage his time and priorities, and self-monitor. As a result, we sometimes served as his "executive secretaries," helping him to stay focused and organized. As a child, we rarely knew how he felt, even when he had been bullied or when depressed or anxious. As an adult, the very same issues were exasperated by his growing social isolation.

Tamika: Tell us about the genesis of Aspiritech.

Brenda: *My husband, Moshe, and I created Aspiritech for Oran. Aspiritech was founded in 2008 with the dream of finding appropriate employment for our son. After* graduating college, finding a suitable, long-term position seemed nearly impossible. Most of the jobs that were found for him were jobs that didn't fit with his skills. His organizational and motor skills challenges made him less suited for manual labor while his social demeanor made it impossible to get an opportunity at jobs that matched his strong intellectual abilities. Though he typically learned new jobs quickly, he could have benefited from some ongoing support when misunderstandings or challenges in the workplace arose, but it wasn't available. Vocational rehab provided at most ninety days of support. We quickly learned that he was not alone, and we didn't want others to go through the same struggles that Oran did, so we made it our mission to create a business that could provide him and other autistic adults the opportunity to realize their potential through gainful and meaningful employment.

After learning about a company in Denmark that employed autistic adults in software QA testing, my husband, Moshe, and I had our answer. Our company name, Aspiritech, was derived from "Asperger's" (the term used at the time) and "technology."

Tamika: Love it—your son was the inspiration behind Aspiritech! Can you talk about how you and your husband worked together as cofounders? Did you have strengths that complemented each other?

Brenda: *I started the company first and Moshe jumped in shortly afterward. Since Moshe is a PhD* *scientist, he is much more "left-brained," analytical, and technical. He was able to handle the QA operations and built the technological components of the company from the ground up. I had worked in the not-for-profit world most of my life and I came from the social service management field, particularly in family support and early child development. At the time, I handled the non-profit, fundraising, support services, and general administration aspects as I had more experience in these sectors. We are definitely "yin and yang" because we are polar opposites. But somehow, our strengths complemented each other, although, at times, our dual leadership has been challenging for us and for our team!*

Tamika: I definitely understand the whole yin and yang thing, that's exactly how I describe Hugo and me. We started a franchise in 2007 and in the initial year it almost cost us our marriage until we realized we had different strengths and then started doing the work that focused on our strengths. But can you give our readers some even deeper insight into how Aspiritech started?

Brenda: *In October of 2007, after learning that our son had lost another job, I decided that something needed to be done. I wrote to every single professor I could find online at the Kellogg School of Management of Northwestern University for help to develop a business plan for an autism employment project. I wrote up the issues around autism employment as I then saw them.*

Every single professor responded respectfully. I had an initial idea of my husband working with my son on developing a website, as Oran is a good writer with specific interests around video games, entertainment, and books. I wasn't thinking at the time much beyond our son and maybe a few other employees. I definitely didn't imagine a company with more than 120 people and with Aspiritech blazing a trail for the community! My focus was on the business case—how the strengths of autism can be an asset. Dr. Temple Grandin speaks a lot more eloquently about that, but anyway . . . Later that year, in December 2007, Marianne Woodward, a professor of social entrepreneurship wrote me back to say, "We're taking you on!" I was shocked! While her brilliant MBA students were researching my small autism employment project (and offered critical suggestions to me), I happened upon The Complete Guide to Asperger's Syndrome by Tony Attwood and found one sentence towards the back that described a Danish company, Specialisterne, founded to employ autistic individuals. That sparked me to start looking into the connection between tech work and the unique strengths and abilities of my son and others like him. Later that year, I also had the fortune of being introduced to another Kellogg MBA student on a similar mission. Japanese student Keita Suzuki was looking to create a similar enterprise because his own young son had been diagnosed right before he had arrived in the United

States. He was tremendously helpful to us in developing the original business model and he even returned to the States in 2009 to help my husband launch a pilot project with our son and another young man whose mother is an advisor to us from our home office dining room. (Keita went on to found his own company, Kaien, in Japan.)

Tamika: That is fascinating. Thank you for sharing so much detail about the inception of Aspiritech. As a founder of a nonprofit myself, and knowing the challenges we can face especially in the beginning, what were some of the initial challenges?

Brenda: *We founded Aspiritech in a time of deep financial crisis. One of the biggest initial challenges was securing seed funding. We struggled with this for a couple of years. At the time, there seemed to be little awareness of the needs of autistic adults or any focus on their strengths and abilities. Few believed that what we were trying to advocate for was worth investing in or were in the position to do so. My husband was able to learn software testing and volunteered to lead the company for the first three years. We wouldn't have Aspiritech if he hadn't done that. I volunteered as executive director for the first six years but still kept my full-time non-profit job. I initially helped part-time (weekends and evenings) with human resources, finances, grant writing, and fundraising. As parents, one does what one needs to do. Truthfully, I wasn't sure what the future would hold for Aspiritech, but we never allowed ourselves to give up hope.*

When we started, the neurodiversity at work movement didn't exist so we were paving the way. At first, securing client business was challenging because companies didn't seem to understand autism or our model and we needed proof of concept. We survived on philanthropy. We had trouble convincing companies that autistic individuals have a unique skill set that could be really beneficial to the business world. It was challenging to get enough business in the door to keep our staff hopeful and gainfully employed.

Not being polished business professionals ourselves didn't help either. We didn't have MBAs; instead, we were a scientist dad and a not-for-profit manager mom. We were truly a mom-and-pop business! But we are thankful for the angels who helped us along the way, starting with our friends, a few philanthropic foundations, and initial board members and volunteers. Our staff were the true pioneers. When people ask why we incorporated as a not-for-profit, I say, one: That's all I knew. And two: I would never recommend leaving monetary resources on the table. We would not have survived back then and be thriving today were we not incorporated as a 501c3. It wasn't until 2014 that we turned the corner, and our business revenue took off.

Tamika: Who helped you along the way?

Brenda: We've had many different angels who have helped us along the way, whether it was individual donors or foundations, media sources, or people who shared their skills and expertise through board membership, volunteerism, or by becoming advisors. It is hard to be unable to name them all, but of special note is a dear friend, Louise Pearson, who has provided much pro bono legal counsel and direct financial support to us over the years.

Our staff has always been the key to our success. Today, all of our QA leads and QA managers are neurodivergent/autistic and we are proud that they were promoted from within. Others who have worked for Aspiritech have moved on but used their training and experience with us as a stepping stone to careers at other companies.

We're proud of many things. We've been leaders in many ways, and we've advised and helped others where and when we could. We are one of the founding members of Neurowrx, a global alliance of companies like Aspiritech, and we are members of the Neurodiversity at Work Employer Roundtable with other companies that include Microsoft and SAP. It's rewarding to see the growth in the number and range of companies, large, midsize, and small. And not all of them are in the technology sector either. These companies are committed to sharing their expertise and often, their intellectual property because everyone is devoted to the overarching mission: propelling employment/supporting employment opportunities/ growing employment opportunities for neurodivergent individuals. Back in 2008, we heard that 90 percent of people on the autism spectrum were either unemployed or severely underemployed and I think that stat is now down to 84 percent. We have made much progress, but still have a very long way to go. For me, this has always been about equal rights and equity issues.

If I had to do it over again, I would try to reach out and get more collaborators from the beginning, because it was hard to build momentum at the start.

I am proud of two recent milestones. First, we bought a headquarters in Evanston, Illinois. It is gorgeous and will become a place that will shine a spotlight on neurodiversity and on the power of networking and collaboration. That's been a long-term dream. Owning our own building also secures our future as it reduces our fixed rent costs, enabling us to invest more of our earnings back into our staff and programs.

Second is the expansion of our training programs. We are developing and piloting Aspiritech Remote Employment Academy (AREA). We are developing e-learning curricula to expand vocational training and employment opportunities for autistic individuals anywhere.

I believe there needs to be a spectrum of vocational opportunities. Not everyone is interested in or best at technology work. What one job is right for everyone in the world? There are so many areas where autistics can contribute and really make a tremendous impact. In addition, we need work to be available in both stand-alone companies, like ourselves and, actually, in every company setting.

Tamika: OK, this leads me to another question: I know Aspiritech originated in your basement, then grew into a small location, and eventually gained a second location. In that growth, you realized that you needed to create this career path within Aspiritech so that you weren't losing these very valuable employees.

Brenda: *In the beginning, we couldn't offer a career path for our employees. But, as we grew, work exploded. Today we work on at least forty-five different projects for dozens of clients. We need leads for each project, and we quickly learned that it was best to tap into our staff who had already demonstrated their success and capabilities and promote them to lead positions. And as we continued to grow, we promoted leads into QA manager positions.*

In addition, because of COVID-19, we shifted to work remotely from home and now we have a hybrid model. We had to learn how to support, train, accommodate and provide social opportunities remotely. It was a huge pivot for us. Most staff were very successful, some not as much. A lot of people, both neurotypical and neurodivergent, have struggled during the pandemic because of stress, anxiety, disruption of routines, and isolation. But one of the things that we learned was that this created an opportunity to train and employ autistics who wanted to work for us from anywhere. Thanks to a grant, we took our introduction to QA training course and created e-learning modules. We hired a training director with seventeen years' experience and a PhD in instructional design. In coordination with our QA and our support experts, she has created phenomenal e-learning units focused on both technical and soft skills development.

What is even more awesome is that participants won't necessarily need to come work for us after they successfully complete the training. They will get a certificate and can take their experience anywhere. And guess what? The Neurodiversity at Work Employer Roundtable just built a neurodiverse career connector and it's just being beta tested. Hats off to Neil Barnett (Director of Inclusive Hiring and Accessibility at Microsoft) and the Roundtable for getting this going!

Tamika: Wow. It's exciting to hear all of the great behind-the-scenes work that we don't often get to hear about and just knowing that more organizations are investing in neurodiversity in the workplace is encouraging. In your opinion, how far has society as a whole come with regard to autism acceptance and a neurodiverse workforce?

Brenda: *There has been a big shift from when we started the company, but we still have a long way to go. Corporations and foundations are increasingly committed* to diversity, equity, and inclusion (DEI), but not all are aware that neurodiversity is a key and critical form of diversity.

Tamika: After fifteen years of leading Aspiritech, one of the country's largest employers of autistic individuals in technology, you and Moshe officially retire at the end of April 2022. What hopes do you see for the future of Aspiritech?

Brenda: *To continue to grow and thrive and stay true to our core mission, values, and vision. There is still so much need. Post-COVID, we expect Aspiritech to once again expand rapidly and to provide vocational training, internships, and employment to as many neurodivergent people as possible. We also expect Aspiritech to expand to other lines of business and for our new headquarters to become a true neurodiversity hub for the community.*

Tamika: What resources have shaped your work and continue to help you?

Brenda: *Our client companies are our No. 1 resource because ninety percent or more of our budget revenue comes from the work we do. Increased client work translates into more positions, with better pay and benefits.*

We also have seen a huge evolution in the resources available to us around autism and employment. This includes lifespan research out of Drexel University and other institutes, the work shared by our professional networks mentioned before, and the voices of self-advocates who help us better understand the world from their perspective. Our nomenclature, values, and focus on neurodiversity, rather than just autism, have changed, too.

Tamika: What barriers/challenges do you see that still exist in our world today?

Brenda: *One of the biggest barriers seems to be reaching and providing equitable services and opportunities to autistic individuals of color, especially those from underserved communities. Moreover, many of our autistic staff are LGBTQIA+, which also creates additional challenges for them.*

Our vision is a world that embraces neurodiversity by recognizing talents, supporting challenges, and welcoming differences. We have to understand that every human being is a spectrum of strengths, challenges, and possibilities and that neurodiversity is a hallmark of the human condition.

Tamika: What advice would you offer to parents of autistic children?

Brenda: *Like so many parents, I personally do not believe I did my best. So few resources were available and knowledge about the spectrum was limited. Overall, it is hard to see your children for who they truly are, whether neurotypical or neurodivergent, but it's what we need to do to be able to help them become their best selves and support their aspirations about who they want to become.*

As a society, we can do better and must do better! We cannot afford to waste talents and have capable individuals fall through the cracks as our son once did.

Tamika: Amen! Last question, if someone wanted to create something similar what advice or warnings would you give them?

Brenda: *Don't do it on your own. Find partners—it's critical. Most important: get neurodivergent people involved to help build your company. And do your best to truly hear them out. Get as many people with diverse skills, backgrounds, and abilities "on your bus." Include autistic self-advocates on your board to lend their voices and perspectives. That saying from Autistic Self Advocacy Network (ASAN), "Nothing about us, without us" is critical.*

Remember that we need a range of vocational opportunities for neurodivergent individuals. They don't all have to be in tech; they can be in the arts or anything else. The sky's the limit. That's why I love the idea of a neurodiversity incubator where individuals might start or grow their own businesses. We (and that includes me!) must stop trying to pigeonhole people into available jobs and begin looking at what jobs align with an individuals' strengths, challenges, and interests. If we can transform how we view employment for autistics, just think how much productivity and other incremental costs we could reduce, redirect, or avoid. And remember, neurodiversity drives innovation. We need a spectrum of opportunities for those on the spectrum. Our world needs people who can think outside the box!

Tamika: Thank you, Brenda, for your time. This has been great! I thank you and Moshe for daring to dream and take action. May this interview serve as inspiration for individuals and organizations alike.

Resources
Self-Advocacy:
- Self-advocates/researchers/thought leaders I like to follow:
  - Lutza Ireland, PhD, www.linkedin.com/in/dr-lutza-ireland-5b028116b/?originalSubdomain=au
  - John Elder Robison, jerobison.blogspot.com
  - Stephen Shore, EdD, drstephenshore.com
  - Temple Grandin, PhD, templegrandin.com
  - Dr. Tony Attwood, tonyattwood.com.au
- ASAN Autistic Self-Advocacy Network, autisticadvocacy.org
- Autistic Women and Non-Binary Network (AWN), awnnetwork.org/wp-content/uploads/2019/05/AWNNetworkParentPacket.pdf

Neurodiversity
- Neurodiversity Network, neurodiversitynetwork.net/neurodivergent-leaders

Career and Self Development
- Neurodiversity Career Connector, ndcc.simplifyhire.com

- Neurodiversity Network, neurodiversitynetwork. net/career-self-development

Networks for Employers and Advocates:

- Neurowrx, a global alliance to accelerate the employment of autistics in STEM, neurowrx.org
- Neurodiversity @ Work Employer Roundtable, a collection of employers committed to neurodiversity-focused hiring initiatives, disabilityin.org/what-we-do/committees/neurodiversity-at-work-roundtable

Vocational Training

- Aspiritech AREA program: Aspiritech Remote Employment Academy funded by Mitsubishi Electric America Foundation offers training and summer internships in Intro to QA (Quality Assurance), soft skills, and more—in process! AREA@aspiritech.org

Email: info@aspiritech.org
Website: aspiritech.org

Social Media

Facebook/ Instagram/ LinkedIn/ Twitter/ YouTube: Aspiritech

Hashtags

#StrongerTogether#Aspiritech
#NeurodiversityDrivesInnovation

My Love Letter to My Team

Dear Aspiritech Team Members,

After fifteen years at Aspiritech, Moshe and I, co-founders, are about to retire. We are so proud of what Aspiritech has become and we have been amazed at its journey thus far. From its birth during the 2008 financial crisis, a time when few recognized the need for increased opportunities for autistic adults, Aspiritech has endured and become a leader in our field. More recently, we survived and even thrived despite the pandemic. We have no doubt that Aspiritech will be in the best of hands going forward and cannot wait to see all that the future holds for our pioneering, social enterprise.

Back in 2008, I named our fledgling business Aspiritech by combining Asperger's and technology. (The nomenclature has certainly changed!) We played with the consonants in "asper" and "tech" and suddenly the letters SPRT emerged. Aspiritech's name and logo highlight the term "spirit," synonymous with "strength, courage, fortitude, guts, and character." These are qualities descriptive of all of you—autistic and neurodivergent adults, who, despite the challenges of living in a neurotypical world and workplace, aspire each and every day to attain fulfilling and meaningful lives. You have important talents and abilities to share with the world. Please do not ever forget that!

Aspiritech's continuing success is first and foremost because of you, its neurodivergent team members. You are at the heart of all that Aspiritech does. We are so indebted to you for all we have learned over the years. The neurodiversity at work movement has grown and evolved, in large part, because of your dedication. There is so much more to accomplish, but, given your spirit and tenacity, we can retire with great confidence in what the future holds.

With love and respect,
Brenda

BIOGRAPHY

Brenda Weitzberg is the executive director and co-founder of Aspiritech. She has a bachelor's degree in psychology and special education with a graduate diploma in administration. She has more than forty years' experience in social service administration, including as director of north shore operations for a Chicagoland nonprofit.

Throughout the years, Brenda has successfully worked collaboratively to develop and implement innovative programs to meet urgent community needs, including Camp STAR, an evidence-based summer treatment program for children with ADHD, ASD, and related disorders.

About the Author

TAMIKA LECHEÉ MORALES

Teacher, actress, author, speaker, entrepreneur, and president of The Autism Hero Project (AHP), a nonprofit organization after her own heart.

Comcast Newsmakers, Fox News, NBC, Univision, Telemundo, and WGN9–Chicago's Very Own are just a few of the media outlets that have featured this "Firessa." Tamika's commitment to community inspired the very first *Today's Inspired Latina Woman of the Year Award* in 2018 and the 2020 *Wintrust Bank Superhero Community Award.*

When Tamika is not serving her community primarily as a second-grade dual language teacher, she serves the autism community as president and director of the board for The Autism Hero Project (AHP), a nonprofit organization that is dedicated to "preparing kids with autism for the world and preparing the world for them." AHP does more than just raise awareness and compassion for families and children on the autism spectrum. These heroes are intentional about creating a world of inclusion and sponsor medical insurance for children on the spectrum to gain access to the therapies they need to thrive and unlock their full potential.

As an actress, Tamika has been fortunate to play several leading roles by inspiring Latinx playwrights. Tamika is passionate about serving humanity by raising cultural awareness, invoking thought, and activating consciousness in the hearts and minds of audiences. Her acting career became the catalyst for sharing her life stories as a playwright and co-author for the book series, *Today's Inspired Latina Volume III: Life Stories of Success in the Face of Adversity*, published in May 2017, and her story "Heroes Wanted" in *Hispanic Stars Rising: The New Face of Power* released in November 2020. Also, her book, Inclusion, was released in December 2021.

Tamika is on a personal mission to enjoy life to the fullest and relishes doing it with the people she loves most, family and friends.

Tamika Lecheé Morales
Email: the.nuyorican.play@gmail.com
Website: www.fortheloveofautism.com
www.tamikamorales.com

Social Media
Facebook: TheNuyorican
Instagram: the_nuyorican_tamika
LinkedIn: Tamika Lecheé Morales
Twitter: TheNuyorican
TickTok: the_nuyorican_tamika
YouTube: Tamika Lecheé Morales

The Autism Hero Project
Email: Autismheroproject@gmail.com
Website: www.autismheroproject.org

Social Media
Facebook: autismheroproject
Instagram: autismheroproject
LinkedIn: the-autism-hero-project
TikTok: AutismHeroProject
Twitter: AutismHero_AHP
YouTube: Autism Hero Project

Made in the USA
Middletown, DE
28 April 2022

64856072R00189